Dangerous Emotions

Dangerous Emotions

Alphonso Lingis

× × × × × × × × × × × × × × ×

UNIVERSITY OF CALIFORNIA PRESS

Berkeley / Los Angeles / London

Chapter twelve's opening illustration is printed with the permission of JuJu Films, Inc. Photo by Malcolm Hearn. All other photographs are by the author.

University of California Press
Berkeley and Los Angeles, California

University of California Press, Ltd.
London, England

© 2000 by
The Regents of the University of California

Library of Congress Cataloging-in-Publication Data

Lingis, Alphonso, 1933–
    Dangerous emotions/Alphonso Lingis.
      p.   cm.
    Includes bibliographical references.
    ISBN 0-520-21629-6 (alk. paper). — ISBN 0-520-22559-7 (pbk.: alk. paper)
    1. Emotions (Philosophy)   I. Title.
  B945.L4583 D36 2000
  128'.37—dc21
                                        99-045371

Printed in the United States of America
9 8 7 6 5 4 3 2 1

The paper used in this publication meets the minimum requirements of American National Standard for Information Sciences—Permanence of Paper for Printed Library Materials, ANSI Z39.48-1984.

Contents

1

The Navel
of the World

Te Pito O Te Henua, the Navel of the World, is the most
isolated inhabited island there is, thirty-six hundred kilometers from the South American coast, two thousand
kilometers from the nearest inhabited island—tiny Pit-
cairn, where the mutineers from the *Bounty* settled with
their Tahitian women. It is thirteen miles long and at its
widest point seven and eight tenths, a pebble in the vast
Pacific. Its low rhythmic profile is the result of three volcanic rises from the ocean floor—three million, one million, and six hundred thousand years ago—connected by
secondary volcanic cones. There are no rivers, no bays,
and no coral reefs about the island. Three volcanic craters
contain lakes of rain water. Most of the surface is strewn
with black chunks of jagged lava. Here and there are expanses of built-up topsoil a few feet thick. Once mantled
with tropical forest, the island has long been treeless, and
today only a few planted eucalyptus groves stand here and
there to ripple the trade winds that constantly blow east-
ward. The entire population of the island—two thousand
five hundred, half Chilean, half now mostly mestizo natives—have been settled in the one village, Hanga Roa.
In this season, the rains are beginning with intermittent
drizzle and so the island is green. Tourists come—only
some four thousand a year—in the dry season and for the
"Easter Island Week," when the locals put on a "native"
show. There descended from our Tahiti-bound plane the
inevitable group of Japanese tourists I would occasionally
see in the days that followed, seated in their bus with
their Japanese guide, and a few stragglers as solitary as I:

when we happened to arrive at the same site, one turned away to contemplate the horizon until the other left. I stayed in a room in the house of a very old couple who spoke hardly any Spanish.

A living organism is a dense and self-maintaining plenum. Out of the energies it assimilates from its environment it generates forces in excess of what it needs to adjust to that environment and compensate for the intermittent and superficial lacks produced by evaporation and fuel consumption. The discharges of these superabundant forces are felt in passions. But the environment itself is full of free and nonteleological energies—trade winds and storms, oceans streaming over three-fourths of the planet, drifting continental plates, cordilleras of the deep that erupt in volcanic explosions, and miles-deep glaciers piled up on Antarctica that flow into the sea and break off in bobbling icemountains. How can the passions of penguins, albatrosses, jaguars, and humans not lift their eyes beyond the nests and the lairs and the horizons? How can these passions not sink into volcanic rock and the oceanic deserts?

When you are there you have the impression you will stay indefinitely. The extinct volcanoes have settled into a placid harmony of low, grass-covered cones in the balmy mist. Along its edges the island drops in sharp lava shards whipped by the waves; beyond there is the shimmering blue. From the top of any of its rises, you see the ocean all around and the curvature of Earth. Above, the clouds thin out and the sun illuminates limitless depths of sky. There are two hundred forty long, low stone altars spaced all along the edges of the island, a thousand giant stone statues, and some fifteen thousand other archaeological sites—remains of dwellings, petroglyphs, caves.

But it is nothing like visiting a vast, open-air museum, inspecting the details and decoding the significance of a thousand works of art. All the giant statues have been hurled from their altars since that Easter Day in 1722. All the smaller statues and carvings have been removed by collectors and tourists; the tiny museum has only copies. Thor Heyerdahl's account of his plunder is in *Aku-Aku*, a sickening book. Only in four sites have the statues, mostly broken, been re-erected in recent times. Called *moai*, the monolithic statues were carved over a fourteen-hundred-year period. They are remarkably uniform, all very stylized busts of legendary ancestors. Out of a thousand, three are vaguely female.

Mostly you walk, led on by the grassy harmony of the island, and at a site you rest and enter a kind of empty revery over the crumbled altars and the broken moai fallen face forward over the rubble.

When you come upon one of the four restored sites, you find five or seven moai, cemented back together where possible, very worn by the wind and the elements and the centuries. The head of a moai is as big as its chest, and it has no feet; the thin arms and long fingers are traced in relief over the abdomen, always in the same position. The head, very flat, is really just a face, with low forehead, sharp, square jaw, thin, tight lips, a strong nose with wide-open nostrils carved in a spiral, and huge empty eyes. The face is turned upward somewhat; the eyes do not, like the eyes of the Buddha, look compassionately on the people below. They look inward to the island, and over the low grassy width of the island to the ocean beyond. They are the depersonalized faces of the legendary chiefs who fifteen hundred years ago sailed four thousand kilometers and disembarked on this volcanic crust. Stern, hieratic, rigid, uniform, these figures certainly impose a severe order on the inhabitants, and anthropologists indeed say that early Polynesian society was very structured. But surely their great size—twelve

to thirty feet high—and their eyes fixed expressionless
and unbenevolent on remoteness beyond the horizon, demanded and commanded their passions. To the wanderer
among them today, these huge empty eyes fixed on horizons beyond this island, beyond any visible horizon, rule
one's every, increasingly aimless, step. With their jaws
designed by geometry, their thin, tight lips, the only ani-
mation on these faces is in their strong splayed nostrils,
pulling in the forces of the winds.

The "mystery" of this island, kept up by anthropologists applying for funding, by travel writers and tourist
brochures, was created by the Westerners who came
upon the island, saw the statues, looked at the islanders,
and concluded that the present inhabitants could not
have created the statues, that they were the work of a
lost civilization colonized from Egypt, Greece, India, the
lost continent of Mu, or outer space. How were the statues transported on this island that had neither trees
nor vines that could serve as ropes? There were no pack
animals, indeed no mammals at all on the island, nor
wheels. The islanders had no metallurgy, no pottery, no
weaving. They lived on the edge of the sea and fished
and cultivated gardens of sweet potato, taro, and bananas.
They wore no clothing and instead covered their bodies
with tattoos. Missionaries labeled the people cannibals.
Thor Heyerdahl was struck by how the altars are made
of separately carved and polished stones fitted together
into jigsaw walls as perfect as those of Qosqo, and he
sailed the Kon-Tiki to prove that the island was colonized
by people from Inca Peru. By the islanders' own account,
Hotu Matu'a had set sail with three hundred of his people fleeing volcanic eruptions in their homeland, the islands those who live there call Te Fenua Enata—"The
Land of Men," which we today call the Marquesas. It has
only been in the past thirty years that archaeologists got

around to determining that the island had been settled around A.D. 300 by a people who began carving statues almost at once. When the Europeans first came upon them, there were hundreds of enormous statues being carved in the quarry, one sixty-five feet tall weighing three hundred tons. The language of the islanders has been found to be akin to that of the Marquesas, four thousand kilometers to the west, and blood and gene sampling has shown no evidence of migrations from other places. The islanders clearly had very advanced navigational science, steered by the stars, had knowledge of sea currents, observed the flight patterns of birds, and must subsequently have gone on to the South American continent, since their staple food, the sweet potato, has never been found growing wild anywhere outside South America. They alone, of all the peoples of the Pacific, invented writing, *rongo-rongo*, partly phonetic and partly ideographic, and inscribed it on wood tablets. Every house had such tablets, and each year there were two competitions in which learned scholars chanted the contents of their tablets before the king and the whole people. The history, cosmology, and science of the islanders became a mystery in the nineteenth century, when the population was enslaved and decimated, the few survivors were Christianized, and the surviving twenty-one pieces of this writing, taken by collectors to Rome, Venice, and Petrograd, became undecipherable.

The volcano Rano Raraku rises out of a flat landscape near the edge of the sea. Virtually all of the thousand giant moai of the island were quarried out of the yellow stone of its crater wall. In that crater wall today there are three hundred ninety-four statues in all stages of completion. First the face, then the abdomen were carved and polished, with stones of lapilli, until the statue was attached only by the rib of the spine. Recent experiments have shown it would take at least a year for a team of men to carve a small moai. When a moai was finished—save for the eyes—it was cut free, slid down the mountain, and set upright. Those carved inside the crater were moved out through a passage cut in one side of the crater wall. Some seventy-five moai lie fully completed at the base of the volcano; these have been covered up to the neck by the erosion from the mountain over the last two hundred years. A half-dozen lie face down on the way to their final locations.

Recent experiments to move them with sledges or fulcrums only showed that the moai would have been ground down by the rubble on the way. It is possible that they were actually carried on the backs of hundreds of assembled people, then somehow set upright.

The red topknots were quarried inside the Puna Pau volcano, then somehow rolled out of the crater, and finally somehow hoisted up onto the statues; many weigh ten tons. When the statues were erected on their altars on the edge of the sea, the eyes were carved and their gaze directed into distances beyond all things to see or messages to capture.

Heyerdahl dug out the buildup of dirt from the completed statues at the base of the volcano to expose them; they have since been covered back up to preserve them. In Cairo ten years ago, in the museum, I saw all the mummies, torn out of their tombs, stripped of their flowers and gods, and laid out in plain wood cases under glass with their blackened faces exposed; on the walls an American scientist had put his X-ray photos of their skeletons, and the urn containing the entrails of Queen Hapshetshut was split open and brightly illuminated. Rano Raraku is a quarry of works in progress. Should we now dig out these moai and erect them on rebuilt altars? Philosophy too consists of works in progress, cut short by

the death of innumerable philosophers. Should we, using
Merleau-Ponty's working notes, write the rest of *The
Visible and the Invisible* for him? Should we complete
Mahler's Tenth Symphony?

The crater walls are very steep; from the top you see
the blue ocean beyond extending to the sky, which you
then find reflected on the lake within. Only one side of
the crater was being carved, but there moai were emerging head up, head down—not a foot of rock that was not
taking on form. The sea is eroding its way toward this
side of the crater, but if the carving had continued the
volcano would have been carved away before the waves
of the ocean arrived. At the base of the volcano, only the
heads of the completed moai are seen, bent over and
blind, their bodies covered to the neck by the mountain
that has eroded from above upon them. I spent two long
afternoons among them, alone save for one hawk soaring
above. It understood, perhaps, that I was waiting for my
death.

After apparently living for fourteen hundred years on
the Navel of the World unknown to the world, God, or
themselves, the islanders were discovered by the Dutch
captain Jacob Roggeveen on Easter Day in 1722. Captain
Roggeveen named the island Easter Island, shot dead
thirteen and wounded many more of the inhabitants
who welcomed him, and left the next day stocked up
with foodstuffs. In 1770 Captain Don Felipe González
came upon the island, disembarked with two priests and
a battalion of soldiers, who advanced in formation to the
center of the island. He named it Isla de San Carlos,
forced some natives to sign in their rongo-rongo script a
Spanish document addressed to King Carlos III beseech-
ing to be annexed by Spain, and left. In 1774 Captain
Cook arrived, and stayed three days. He sent his men to
search the whole island; they found only a hundred men

and no women or children, shot one native for touching
an officer's bag, forced the others to load up baskets with
potatoes for the scurvy-infected ship, and set sail again.
On the ship the sailors found the baskets filled with
stones under a covering of potatoes. In 1786 a French
warship under le Comte de la Pérouse stopped at the island for eleven hours; the cove where the warship an-
chored is "honored" today with his name. An unrecorded
number of pirates, whalers, and sealers also came upon
the island; one whose visit was recorded was the American sealer *Nancy*, whose captain set out in 1805 to capture the natives for slavery on his Juan Fernandez island
base. He was able to capture only twelve men and ten
women. After three days at sea, he untied them; they all
leapt overboard and drowned. He returned to the island
to round up more. In 1822 the men of an American
whaler, the *Pindos*, rounded up island women to take
with them; they later threw them into the sea and shot at
them. On the island syphilis and leprosy spread. Starting
in 1859 slave traders regularly raided the island. In 1862
an armada of seven Peruvian ships commanded by Captain Aiguirre was able to capture two hundred men for
slavery in the guano mines of Peru. Eighteen more slave
ships came in the following year. Under pressure from
the French administrators of Tahiti and the English, the
Peruvian authorities ultimately agreed to repatriate
these slaves. Only a hundred were still alive; of these
eighty-five died on the return voyage, and the fifteen
who disembarked were infected with smallpox which
decimated the island. All the giant statues of the island
were hurled from their altars between 1722 and 1864. A
Catholic missionary was brought in, the people were converted, the rongo-rongo tablets burnt, and family collec-
tions of heirlooms, statues, and wood carvings, said now
to be the work of demons, were destroyed. The mission-

ary also brought in tuberculosis. In 1888 Chile annexed the island, rounded up the remaining population of one hundred eleven, put them in a barbed-wire corral at Hanga Roa, and allotted the rest of the island to sheep ranchers. Few Chileans were interested; it was British who bought the ranching concessions and turned the island over to seventy thousand sheep, which denuded the island of its shrubbery and chewed the grass to the roots. Too distant for economically feasible transportation, the sheep were eliminated in recent years and replaced by horses and cattle owned by two Chilean corporations. In 1934 the French anthropologist Alfred Métraux made the first cultural exploration of the island; the Chilean government was persuaded of its tourist possibilities and in 1935 made most of the coastline a national park. In 1986, after the explosion of the Challenger, the American space program NASA built an airstrip on the island for the recovery of satellites falling into the Pacific.

About halfway through grade school I brought up a linguistic problem to the teacher. She—and the textbook—called the Roman civilization a great civilization. It was said to be at its greatest when its military dominated the greatest number of lands and peoples. When its empire shrank, it was said to be in decline. This terminology persisted in history class after history class throughout my schooling, and in museum after museum I have visited since. The great religions are the world religions. Civilization advances with military and economic expansionism. A euphemism is competition: without competition there is no artistic, literary, or religious advance. (Without grades, prizes, honors, there is no philosophical achievement.) My first trip was to Florence, where I was beset by the evidence that its grand artistic, literary, and musical achievements coincided with its richest and most rapacious century; as soon as that century was over, Florence could only sigh on in mannerism. Today Florence is rich through tourism, but without political expansionism its artistic and literary culture is comparable to that of Oklahoma City. Culture is the glory of a civilization that rises in the glint of advancing swords and cannon. The frantic theories of Thor Heyerdahl and the others striving to prove that the sculpture and the altar walls on Te Pito O Te Henua show cultural imports from Inca Peru, from Egypt, Greece, India, or China are based on the conviction that an isolated culture always declines.

I crisscrossed Te Pito O Te Henua many times, exploring this crust of volcanic cinders covered with grass, ending up inevitably at the featureless sea and the curvature of Earth beneath the unending flow of wind and sky. The small flowers in the grass you see everywhere: the island has but thirty species of indigenous plantlife. There are no coral reefs swarming with fish to attract sea birds and sea mammals. The few sparrows and small hawks you see are recent imports. No rodents or lizards scurry through the chunks of lava. There are no cliff fortresses—only the harmonious low cones of volcanos extinct a million years ago. The population of the island stabilized at about fifteen thousand; for fourteen hundred years the rulers continued the hereditary line unbroken from the founder Hotu Matu'a. The statues had already reached gigantic size in the seventh century, and the evolution of their stylization was gradual over the next thousand years. Though the now mute rongorongo books can no longer tell the wanderer of the history, cosmology, and science of this civilization, the statues' great eyes and splayed nostrils tell him of its passion. An obsessive drive, nowise economic or rational, erected these depersonalized stone faces with eyes looking out into the featureless emptiness. The force of this passion was the force of volcanos and the wind and the ocean and the sky.

The southwest end of the island, called Rano Kau, is a four-mile walk up slow-rising, rolling grassland, with many pauses to contemplate the sea and the island. Only when you step over a grassy rim at the top do you suddenly realize that Rano Kau is an extinct volcano: below is a rocky bowl containing a circular lake a mile wide. You walk along the crater rim; the land is a high plateau to your right. When you reach the far side the plateau drops a thousand feet into the ocean; the outer wall of the crater here is a vertical cliff. Below, a few miles away you see three small islands, the first a stalagmite rising abruptly out of the ocean, then two rocky outcroppings. Near the volcano rim on the edge of the cliff, there are boulders covered with petroglyphs—images in high relief of men with bird heads, of vulvas, of faces of the god Makemake. This is the place called Orongo.

Down a short slope from the boulders, along the very edge of the cliff there are fifty-three small buildings. Seen from above they form clusters of grass-covered ovals. When you descend among them, you see that their walls are made of uncemented sheets of slate laid flat and corbeled. The entrances, all facing the ocean, are at ground level, two feet high and so narrow you have to lift one side of your torso to crawl inside. It is the sacred precinct of Mata Ngarau. These are the residences of the priests of the birds. The islands below were the nesting places of the migratory terns, the manu-tara.

Each year when the manu-tara returned, the tangata-manu, the birdmen chosen in dreams by the priests in the sacred precinct, descended the cliff. They swam across the straits to the island called Motu Nui among sharks racing through the wild currents. All the birdmen were strong and brave; chance determined which of them would find the first egg laid. The birdman who was able to return to Mata Ngarau with that first egg had his hair, brows, and eyelashes shaven, carved his birdman image into a boulder, and, as the new king, descended to cross the island to the crater of Rano Raraku, where he would live in complete seclusion among the silent and eyeless moai for the year of his reign. Under his crown of plumage his hair grew, and he did not cut his nails. His food was brought by a servant who took pains not to be seen. On the islands thousands of terns jostled and hatched their eggs; on the cliff above, the people performed entranced orgiastic rites. The reign of the birdman kings was recent, beginning in 1780. During the year, the other birdmen and the priests at Mata Ngarau were paramount throughout the island, not so much ruling as descending upon its settlements in orgiastic raids. It was they Western historians were describing when they wrote that the last period of Easter Island civilization was a time of decadence and anarchy.

The bird culture is the late dominance of an aboriginal stream of this civilization. The founding king Hotu Matu'a who had set sail with the original colonizers in the third century was surely led to this minuscule island by birds. The colonists brought with them poultry, which remained their only domestic animal. They also brought their Marquesas deities, among whom Makemake, the god of the bird culture, gradually became dominant. But for fourteen hundred years the culture was structured, hieratic, under hereditary rulers.

It was in the eighteenth century, when the island became prey to plunderers from the outside, when the thousand-year-old temples were overturned, when the people hid in closed volcanic caves at the first sight of any foreign ship on the horizon, that the period called anarchy by Western writers came about. The ancient

hereditary kings, the last of whom died in slavery in
Peru, were replaced by men whose prowess naked in the
raging sea marked them to be temporary sovereigns. But
their sovereignty was not an administration of a structured society, which now existed no more; he who brought
the first egg of the manu-tara was king, and his sovereignty was as pervasive as he was invisible, until the
terns returned to the sea. What he presided over was
not a panicky totalitarian culture bent on preserving its
sedentary economy from the depredations of yet more
rapacious agents of the mercantile societies of the
Dutch, English, French, Russians, and Peruvians, but,
in its ruins, the liberation of a totally different kind of
culture—a culture of pride, daring and chance, violence
and eroticism. A culture of birds.

The last birdman reigned in 1866; his name was
Rokunga. By 1868 the last pagan on the island had been
baptized by the Picpus missionary Eugène Eyraud.

The migratory terns called manu-tara, of the species
Sterna lunata, no longer return to the island called
Motu Nui.

Historians go back to the individual initiatives and collective enterprises that were undertaken by those now
dead—more exactly, to the texts that recorded those
things and to the monuments, artifacts, and ruins which
are not only described in texts but can be read as texts.
When historians write the text of history, their work is
not so much to inscribe those initiatives and enterprises,
triumphs and defeats themselves, as it is to reinscribe
their meaning. When scholars take a text of Euclid or
Herodotus and set out to determine what it meant, their
first task is to recycle in their brains the thoughts of a
man long dead. Writing exists to make that possible. A
text has surely the meaning it had for the author as he

composed its sentences, but the scholar also sets out to determine the meaning it had for the readers to whom the author addressed it, and for the readers whose conditions, concerns, and values the author could not envision with clarity or certainty, as well as for readers he did not envision at all. The historian's text inscribes not only the meaning the individual initiatives and collective enterprises had for those who launched them, but also the meaning they had for those who celebrated them or defeated them, and the meaning they had for the generations that came later and built and destroyed in the world which those initiatives and enterprises had shaped. And the historian formulates the meaning of the past for his own generation and their descendants. History presumes that we must learn from the deeds, triumphs, and defeats of the past.

From time immemorial people gathered about the fire and told tales of the great deeds, great triumphs, and great defeats of their heroes. In listening to the tales and in reading the chronicles of their people, men and women found their hearts pounding and their brains fevered with the audacities, hopes, loves, and hatreds of heroes and heroines who were dead. The historian may decipher those emotions on the texts, monuments, artifacts, and ruins he finds.

But the modern historian writes dispassionately, neither exulting in the victory of Cortéz nor weeping over the defeat of Moctezoma. He is not writing in order to feel again and make his reader feel again the torrential emotions of men and women long dead. He is not writing to crowd his soul with all the loves and hatreds, despairs and exultations of those who wrought great deeds and those who suffered terrible defeats. He thinks that his contemporaries and their descendants should learn from the lessons of history before launching enterprises and unleashing the passions that will drive them; and he thinks that the lessons are not yet in, the data are fragmentary and so often ambiguous. He knows well that the Spanish and the Mexica drew contradictory conclusions from the fall of Tenochtitlán. And he thinks that if emotions focus the mind, they also limit it. There is an opacity to emotions; they cloud the mind such that it does not see things in their whole context.

Emotions color the line drawings with which cognition represents reality. The philosophical distinction between the cognitive senses and private feelings can be traced back to Aristotle; it continues to our day in the concept of objective scientific knowledge. We take emotions to be distinctively human phenomena. Outside the crystal ball of the human psyche, there are only grass that does not wince when we tread on it, trees that are impassive as the chain-saw slashes them, water that does not shiver with pleasure when we stroke it, atoms drifting through the void without anxiety and colliding without pleasure or pain. If these things move us, it is because we are moved by the colors we project onto them. All colors, according to John Locke and seventeenth-century epistemology, including the "color" of emotion, are subjective effects within the psyche of the viewer.[1]

For Nietzsche, man's glory is to be not the contemplative mirror in which nature is represented but the Dionysian artist who in giving style to his movements makes an artwork out of the most precious clay and oil, his own flesh and blood—and the Apollonian dreamer who gives form to the waters above and the waters below, to the stars and the dry land, to the creeping and crawling things about him. Nietzsche praised as old masters the dancer and dreamer in us whose emotions are a pot of colors.

Emotions are also forces. The grand colors come
from strong surges of prodigal energies within a life.
For Nietzsche emotions are excess energies the organism
produces that overflow those operations with which the
organism adjusts to its environment. Strong surges of energies in the environment itself, disintegrating the placid
order of settled things, are not part of the explanation
for emotional forces. After all, Nietzsche would point out,
a weak, contented or resentful, human and one of exalted, frenzied vitality view the same spectacle—a thunderstorm over the mountains or the ocean waves breaking against the cliffs—differently, and a scientist can
view a flood in Bangladesh or on the Mississippi plain
with dispassionate composure.

The modern philosophy of mind took emotions to
be inner states, experiences with only one witness. One
infers, on the basis of perceived behaviors, that there
are feeling states in others analogous to those one
knows within oneself. No dentist feels his patient's
toothache; everyone can agree on the size and shape
of the Mona Lisa's smile but there is no agreement
about whether that smile is mellifluous or irritatingly
priggish.

Yet what is more evident than the pain of an accident
victim, than the agony of the mother of that victim? At
ten days, a newborn infant recognizes with a smile the
smile of his mother. What is more visible than the glee
of an infant playing with a kitten, and if that infant tod-
dles off into the woods, can there be any doubt about the
joy of the mother when he is found?

The hilarity, the fear, the rage, the relief, the agony,
the desperation, the supplication are what are most visible about those we look at. At a glance we see that the
cop or the office manager is incensed, even though we

find we cannot say later what color his eyes are and had not noticed that she had dyed her hair.

Indeed, the mirth and the despondency, the irritability and the enthusiasm, the rapture and the rage are the very visibility of a body. A body's shape and contours are the way that it is held in a space that excludes other bodies and us; a body's colors are opaque expanses behind which the life-processes are hidden. It is through its feelings, drawing our eyes into their fields of force, that a body emerges out of its self-contained closure and becomes visible. Through the windshield the hitchhiker sees the distrust of the driver of the car. As we walk by trees and figures in the park, it is the pleasure radiating out of the smiling face and the exposed arms and fingers of an old woman feeding pigeons that make us see her. Walking through crowds in the street, we see mortification or heartbreak outlining in relief a middle-aged woman clad in a sensible and ordinary coat.

People poke at mountain goats and reptiles in the zoo; they throw stones at lions. The irritation, the fear, or the anger of the animal are not behind its opaque skin or in its skull; the molester feels the irritation or the anger against his eyes, against the mean smirk on his face. The passerby who sees the irritation, fear, or anger that make the python, fox, or tiger visible—when that emotion is directed against the zookeeper or against another animal—at once feels himself caught up in the range of that passion.

The elations, gaieties, lusts, rancors, miseries, apathies, and despairs of living organisms catch the eyes and hold the attention of passersby. They intrude into the perceptual fields and practical concerns of others. Our emotions reorient others, disturb their trains of thought, seep into the blueprints of their projects, contest them, and afflict them with misgivings and self-doubt. Power among humans is not simply the physical force with which one material body may move another; it is the force to distract, detour, maneuver, and command. Every pleasure we indulge in and every pain we suffer exerts power over others.

We do feel that people who live in flat lands tend to have flat minds and flat feelings, that people who live in cubicles in public housing developments tend to have narrow, constricted feelings. We feel that the objects and landscapes upon which emotions are released can limit the range of emotions that run up against them and eventually cause those feelings to aim at only nearby things.

Not only do emotions discharge their forces on the outside environment; they have their source in it. Was it not the mists and the driving sleet, the blossoming prairies, and the swallows rhapsodic in the tides of summer that opened our hearts to ever more vast expanses of reality, beyond all that is made to content and satisfy us? Rage does not come from nowhere, nor does it come only from the overheating of the organism itself. Love is not a passion felt in human beings alone, nor does it derive from inner needs and wants. Strength and superabundant energies are not generated simply by an inner psychic will that is a will to power. Emotions get their force from the outside, from the swirling winds over the rotating planet, the troubled ocean currents, the clouds hovering over depths of empty outer space, the continental plates shifting and creaking, the volcanos rising from the oceanic abyss, and the nonsensical compositions of mockingbirds, the whimsical fluttering of butterflies in the racket of a wallow of elephant seals. Their

free mobility and energies surge through us; their dis-
quietudes, torments, and outbursts channel through us
as emotions.

People who shut themselves off from the universe
shut themselves up not in themselves but within the
walls of their private property. They do not feel volcanic,
oceanic, hyperborean, and celestial feelings, but only the
torpor closed behind the doors of their apartment or
suburban ranch house, the hysteria of the traffic, and
the agitations of the currency on the stretch of turf they
find for themselves on the twentieth floor of some multinational corporation building.

If one person regards a thunderstorm over the mountains or the ocean waves breaking against the cliffs as
dangerous and another as sublime, the reason is not,
as Immanuel Kant wrote, that the first clings to feeling
the vulnerability of his small body, while the second
initially verifies that his vantage point is safe and then
forms the intellectual concept of infinity, which concept
exalts his mind. And it is not simply, as Nietzsche wrote,
that the first cramps his weak emotional energies back
upon himself, resenting what threatens his security,
while the second has a vitality whose excessive energies
have to be released outside. It is that the first draws his
emotional energies from the forces that hold walls together and closed. A scientist, paid enough to have a
mansion in the suburbs, views the storm from the confines of a laboratory in an earthquake-proof building
where the fluorescent lights never go off during a
thunderstorm. And the second sails the open seas and
the winds, driven by some volcanic eruption in his
Marquesas homeland.

Alone, wandering around Te Pito O Te Henua, I
learned very little. For all its fame, there are not many

books about "Easter Island"—those by Alfred Métraux, Thor Heyerdahl, Jo Anne Van Tilburg, and a few dozen monographs by archaeologists. The few remaining rongo-rongo books are indecipherable; the giant statues are nameless figures of unknown cults. What the islanders believed, what cosmology and myths were the framework within which they carved and transported the giant statues, what cosmogony and epics gave meaning to the recent bird cult, are almost completely lost to us.

Garrulous researchers, who get funded to come to the island to produce a text, set themselves tasks: how many statues are there, how big are they, how much do they weigh? They set out to carbon-date them, classify them according to style, and then try to correlate the statues with kings or gods mentioned in the sparse eighteenth-century sea-captains' logs or with the demons mentioned in the journals of nineteenth-century missionaries.

Yet how one is struck by the depersonalization and repetitiveness of the moai! In Wat Pô, in Bangkok, there is a colonnade that contains a thousand statues, each of the Buddha larger than life size. In Sri Lanka, Myanmar, Thailand, Laos, and Tibet I had seen whole walls of caves carved into statues—all statues of the Buddha, in the same position, genderless, depersonalized. What to make of a whole cave lined with Buddha images all alike?

You do not view the Buddha image as an artwork; you meditate. Your body must be in equilibrium, without any tensions that would produce cramps or shifts. The mind must be empty, so that all thinking, imagining, remembering, speculating will have faded out, leaving you centered on the task of intoning a mantra across the length of a diaphragmic breath. The sacred mantra "OM" means "the Jewel in the Lotus." But the meditator does not think of the meaning or its referent, or if he does, he does so only for the effect it produces. He will intone it again and again, each time more inwardly. Finally the mantra does not resonate outwardly at all. With its simplicity, its sustained purity and endurance,the mantra has become the inner state of his vitality, the still surface of a summer lake so undisturbed that the remote clouds and the shadows of transparent insects can play on it without the least distortion.

The Buddha image is not intended to represent that particular man named Siddhartha Gautama who was born in the Nepalese Himalayas about five hundred years before the Christian era. It is the image of a soul in equilibrium, centered, available for a compassion that is cosmic. The Buddha image is not an icon but a means of meditation, of composing one's forces. Down the corridors of temples and on the walls of caves it is repeated like a mantra.

There is on the giant statues on the rim of the island of Te Pito O Te Henua no trace of the idealized anatomy of Greek anthropomorphized gods, of the haughty sovereignty of Roman emperors, of the sacrificial pathos of Jesus. The moai succeed one another along the edge of the sea and deep in our hearts like mantras. They do not direct us to be on the lookout for another island or for stray ships full of Peruvian gold. They lift our eyes from the surface of the island, and direct our gaze beyond the horizon. Their strong nostrils take in the wind.

I had read all the texts that recent researchers and scholars have written about the statues. But as I wandered from one statue to another, each so like the rest, all these texts faded away. The people who carved them also had put a subtext on them, long ago effaced. I was sure that what I felt, as our texts faded from consciousness, as had theirs long ago, was what, under their subtext, the people who carved the statues and lived among them felt. Walking the volcanic rises of this island and contemplating these broken statues, what these vanished people had felt was clear, palpable, as though I were walking among their very ghosts, as though those ghosts had come to inhabit my nervous circuitry and sensibility. The statues, the very earth, the ocean, the sky, the winds convey what they felt. It was inconceivable that this kind of work, these giant stone statues, could have been erected in the rain forests, or in the temperate latitudes in the middle of continents.

I felt in the vast restlessness of the ocean the profound resolve of these people as they left their Marquesas Islands homeland exploding in volcanic eruptions. I felt in the winds their terror, their bravado, their anxieties during the four thousand kilometers of steering in the uncharted Pacific. I felt in the sea birds' tacking in the trade winds their insomniac trust in the flight of the sea birds that led them here. I felt in the drumming and flash of the surf their exultation at setting foot on the crust of this island. In this navel to which all Earth was reduced, before this vacant ocean, under this empty sky, in the midst of these never-ending east winds, I felt their appetite for life and for reality. In the low grass-covered cones in the balmy mist, I felt the placid harmony of the fourteen hundred years of their work and repose. In the huge eyes of a thousand moai of volcanic stone turned to fathomless distances, I felt their taste for the impossible.

On Te Pito O Te Henua it was clear to me that the passions turned to fathomless distances that raised those stones into giant statues were drawn from the upsurge

of the volcanos themselves, that those vacant eyes reflected the radiance of the skies, that the song of the
winds and the seas was on those lips, and that those great
stone faces and their raiment held the color of the ardent
lava and of the restless oceanic depths.

2

Bestiality

Sea anemones are animated chrysanthemums made of
tentacles. Without sense organs, without a nervous system,
they are all skin, with but one orifice that serves as mouth,
anus, and vagina. Inside, their skin contains little marshes
of algae, ocean plantlets of a species that has come to live
only in them. The tentacles of the anemone place inside
the orifice bits of floating nourishment, but the anemone
cannot absorb them until they are first broken down by its
inner algae garden. When did those algae cease to live in
the open ocean and come to live inside sea anemones?

Hermit crabs do not secrete shells for themselves but
instead lodge their bodies in the shells they find vacated
by the death of other crustaceans. The shells of one
species of hermit crab are covered with a species of sea
anemone. The tentacles of the sea anemones grab the
scraps the crab tears loose when it eats. The sea anemones protect the crab from predator octopods, which are
very sensitive to sea anemone stings. When the hermit
crab outgrows its shell, it locates another empty one. The
sea anemones then leave the old shell and go to attach
themselves onto the new one. The crab waits. How do sea
anemones, blind, without sense organs, know it is time to
move?

Ocean extends over seventy-one percent of Earth's surface, and ninety percent of the ocean is more than three
kilometers deep. Below a depth of three hundred meters,
living beings move in total darkness. Squid that live in the
depths where light penetrates eject clouds of ink to hide
behind before their enemies, but an abyss-dwelling squid,

Heteroteuthis dispar, ejects a cloud of fluid glowing with bioluminescent bacteria to light up the waters before itself and locate prey.

Small nomadic bands of people have long lived in the rain forests of the world. But until recently only two ways had been found for humans to commercialize the rain forest without destroying it: tapping rubber trees and collecting Brazil nuts. Rubber has many essential uses in industry, and Brazil nuts have always commanded good prices on the export market. But there are so many species of trees intermixed in the rain forest that rubber tappers and nut collectors often had to walk for an hour from one tree of a species to the next. It early occurred to settlers to cut down the wild forest and establish plantations of rubber trees and Brazil nut trees. The Brazil nut plantations always failed. The trees grew vigorously, flowered, but never produced any nuts. Only fifteen years ago did biologists figure out why. The Brazil nut flowers can be pollinated by only one species of bee. This bee requires, to feed its larvae, the pollen of one species of orchid, an orchid that does not grow on Brazil nut trees. When did Brazil nut flowers come to shape themselves so as to admit only that one species of bee? What we know as Brazil nuts are kernels which on the tree are enclosed in a very large wooden husk containing hundreds of them. The Brazil nut tree is hardwood, and the husk about its seeds is of wood hard as iron. There is only one beast in Amazonia that has the teeth, and the will, to bore into that husk—an agouti. When it bores through the husk, the agouti eats only some of the seeds. Through the bored hole the remaining seeds are able to get moisture and to push their roots into the ground. Without that rodent, the nuts would be permanently entombed, and Brazil nut trees would have died out long ago.

When did celled life, with nuclei, come to evolve? The microbiologist Lynn Margulis established that chloro-

Bestiality

plasts and mitochondria, the oxygen-processing cellular energy-producers in plants and animals, were originally independent cyanobacteria and proteobacteria that came to live inside the cells of plants and animals. Colonies of microbes evolved separately and then formed the symbiotic systems that are the individual cells, whether of algae or of our bodies.

Human animals live in symbiosis with thousands of species of anaerobic bacteria, six hundred species in our mouths that neutralize the toxins all plants produce to ward off their enemies, four hundred species in our intestines, without which we could not digest and absorb the food we ingest. Some synthesize vitamins, others produce polysaccharides or sugars our bodies need. The number of microbes that colonize our bodies exceeds the number of cells in our bodies by up to a hundredfold. They replicate with their own DNA and RNA and not ours. Macrophages in our bloodstream hunt and devour trillions of bacteria and viruses entering our porous bodies continually: they are the agents that maintain our borders. When did those bacteria take up lodging in our digestive system, these macrophages in our bloodstream?

We also live in symbiosis with rice, wheat, and cornfields, with berry thickets and vegetable patches, and with the nitrogen-fixing bacteria in the soil with which the rootlets of all those plants enter into symbiosis in order to grow and feed the stalks, leaves, and seeds or fruit. We also move and feel in symbiosis with other mammals, birds, reptiles, and fish.

How myopic is the notion that a form is the principle of individuation, or that a substance occupying a place to the exclusion of other substances makes an individual, or that the inner organization, or the self-positing identity of a subject is an entity's principle of individuation! A season, a summer, a wind, a fog, a swarm, an intensity of white at high noon have perfect individuality, though they are neither substances nor subjects. The climate, the wind, a season have a nature and an individuality no different from the bodies that populate them, follow them, sleep and awaken in them.

Let us liberate ourselves from the notion that our body is constituted by the form that makes it an object of observation and manipulation for an outside observer! Let us dissolve the conceptual crust that holds it as a subsisting substance. Let us turn away from the anatomical and physiological mirrors that project it before us as a set of organs and a set of biological or pragmatic functions. Let us see through the simple-mindedness that conceives of the activities of its parts as functionally integrated and conceives it as a discrete unit of life. Let us cease to identify our body with the grammatical concept of a subject or the juridical concept of a subject of decisions and initiatives.

The form and the substance of our bodies are not clay shaped by Jehovah and then driven by his breath; they are coral reefs full of polyps, sponges, gorgonians, and free-swimming macrophages continually stirred by monsoon climates of moist air, blood, and biles.

A pack of wolves, a cacophonous assemblage of starlings in a maple tree when evening falls, a marsh throbbing with frogs, a whole night fizzling with fireflies exert a primal fascination on us. What is fascinated is the multiplicity in us—the human form and the nonhuman, vertebrate and invertebrate, animal and vegetable, the conscious and unconscious movements and intensities in us. Aliens on other planets, galaxies churning out trillions of stars, drops of water showing, under the microscope, billions of squiggling protozoa—these are mesmerizing. What is mesmerized in us are the pulses of solar energy momentarily held and refracted in our crystalline cells, the microorganic movements and intensities in the currents of our inner coral reefs.

Bestiality

Our movements are not spontaneous initiatives launched against masses of inertia; we move in an environment of air currents, rustling trees, and animate bodies. Our movements are stirred by the coursing of our blood, the pulse of the wind, the reedy rhythms of the cicadas in the autumn trees, the whir of passing cars, the bounding of squirrels, and the tense, poised pause of deer. The speeds, slowness, and turns of our movements come from movements we meet about us. Our legs plod with elephantine torpor, decked out fashionably we catwalk, our hands swing with penguin vivacity, our fingers drum with nuthatch insistence, our eyes glide with the wind rustling the flowering prairie.

These movements do not only extend space for us; they surge and ebb in intensity. They are vehement, raging, prying, incandescent, tender, cloying, ardent, lascivious. It is through its irritability, its fear, its rage, its languor, its exuberance that an octopus in the ocean, a rabbit caught in our headlights, a serpent in the grass, a cat on the couch become visible to us. Our movements become irritable with the insistent whine of a mosquito, fearful before the fury of a hornet whose nest we have disturbed, languid with the purring of a cat, exuberant in the sparkling of the coral fish in the tropical surge.

We assign special importance, in everyday life, to purposive or goal-oriented movement. Yet most movements—things that fall, that roll, that collapse, that shift, that settle, that collide with other things, that set other things in motion—are not goal-oriented. How little of the movements of the bodies of octopods frolicking over the reef, of guppies fluttering in the slow currents of the Amazon, of cockatoos flaunting their acrobatics in the vines of New Guinea, of terns of the species *Sterna paradisaea* scrolling up all the latitudes of the planet from Antarctica to the Arctics, of humans is teleological! How little of these movements is programmed by an advance

Bestiality

representation of a goal, a result to be acquired or produced, a final state! Most movements do not get their
meaning from an outside referent envisioned from the
start, and do not get their direction from an end-point, a
goal or a result. Without theme, climax, or denouement,
they extend from the middle, they are durations.

How even less do most movements represent initiatives by which an agent posits and extends its identity!
They are nowise the movements by which a conscious
being seeks to maintain, consolidate, and stabilize itself,
still less to integrate itself.

In the course of the day, our bodies shift, lean, settle;
agitations stir them; most of the movements of our arms
and hands are aimless; our eyes glide in their sockets, continually buoyed up and rocked by the waves of sunlight. So
many of the movements to which we assign goals start by
being just an urge to move, to get the day going, to get out
of the house. We go out for a walk in the streets, a stroll
along the beach, a saunter through the woods. In the Ryongi Zen Garden in Kyoto, for five hundred years each
morning a monk rakes again the sands into waves. His
movements are themselves waves, and leave no traces in
the mind, are lost in the winds that shift the sands as he
moves. A campesina in Guatemala occupies her hands with
the rhythms and periodicity of her knitting as she sits on
the stoop gossiping with her friends. A now old Palestinian
who will never leave the refugee camp watches the children play ball and fingers his prayer beads.

Every purposive movement, when it catches on, loses
sight of its telos and continues as a periodicity with a
force that is not the force of the will launching it and
launching it once again and then again. A carpenter
climbs up the roof to nail shingles; almost at once his
mind lets loose the objective and the rhythm dum-dum-
dum-DUM dum-dum-dum-DUM continues his movements. The force he feels in those movements is not the

force of his deciding will but the vibrant and vital intensity of his muscles on the grip of his smoothly balanced
hammer. The rhythm of his hammering is composed
with the rhythms of the passing wind currents and the
falling leaves, and when he pauses he, alone in the
neighborhood, registers the nearby tapping of a nuthatch
on a tree trunk.

The movements and intensities of our bodies take up
the movements and intensities of toucans and wolves, jel-
lyfish and whales. Psychoanalysis censures as infantile
every intercourse with the other animals, which it so ob-
sessively interprets as representatives of the father and
mother figures of its Oedipal triangle. But we are not aim-
ing at an identification with the other animal. Still less are
we identifying the other animal with another human.

The hand of a child that strokes the dolphin takes in
the surges of exuberance that pulse in its smooth body,
while the dolphin in close contact with the child's face
takes in the human waves of intimacy. A woman riding a
horse pumps with the surges of its impulses, while the
horse's pace incorporates her shifts and pulls. The movements of her body extend speed and retardation, and feel
the thrill of speed and the soothing decompression of
slowing down. These movements extend neither toward
a result nor a development. They are figures of the repe-
tition compulsion; we stroke a calf each night on the
farm, we ride a horse through the woods with the utterly
noncumulative recurrence of orgasm.

Our skunk climbs up on our lap, folds her legs under
her round smooth body, closes her mouth and eyes, and
vibrates a glowing contentment. The postural axis that
lines up our torso and limbs for tasks now relaxes, our
thighs cease to be muscled levers for going places and
turn into a soft warm cushion, our eyes cease to inspect
and observe her and wander soft-focus, and our whole
body becomes a nonfunctional mass where her content-

Bestiality

ment rumbling through it is undifferentiated from its pulsating sensuality.

When we watch the seals glide up and down the rocks and into the sea, we feel the tedium of the bodies we had to evolve when we left the ocean. A hundred seventy pounds, of salty brine mostly, in an unshapely sack of skin: what a clumsy weight to have to transport on our bony legs! We can certainly understand the dolphins and whales, mammals that evolved on land but long ago returned to the ocean. When we return to the ocean, we have to pull a layer of rubber skin over our bodies, strap on a buoyancy compensator, an air tank with regulator and gauges, weight belt, eye mask, and flippers. And then how ludicrous we look when we lurch our bodies equipped with all these prosthetic organs out of the dive shop and wade with flippered feet across the beach till we reach deep water! In the deep, all these supplementary organs only make our species-organs nonfunctional. We abandon our upright posture that we long ago evolved in order to free our hands for grasping, taking, manufacturing, and expressing. The swim-strokes we trained into our bodies to move across the surface of water are useless underwater; we fold our hands under us so as not to stir up the sand in front of our eyes. Our flippered feet take up the wave movements of fish, and we mostly do that only to descend and ascend when our air tank is used up. Underwater any coral head, the most biologically diverse environment on the planet, will occupy our mesmerized eyes the hour we have. We are reduced to just eyes, looking without surveying. We learn nothing, not even how to identify as species of fish the shimmering colors and undulatory forms silently streaking about us; back on the beach, paging through the *Guide Book of Tropical Fishes*, we can't be sure, looking at their static pictures, if what we saw was a Moorish Idol or a Heniochus, called "Poor Man's Moorish Idol." The pub-

lishers have taken to printing their guide books of tropical fishes on plasticized pages bound with plastic rings so
that divers can take them down with them. I used to ask
divemasters what that fish we had seen was, and was put
out that they never seemed to know. It was only later that
I realized, what they realized long ago, that the high-
point of diving is not to distinguish some rare fish but to
be observed by them. It is the pleasure of having a pair
of angelfish accompany you the whole dive, swimming
next to your goggles, peering into everything you stick
your nose into. It is the exhilaration of having the great
shark career by or pause inches from your head, its small
lemon-yellow eye fixed on you. At first it may take some
effort to avoid doing something, trying to drive it off or
to flee. But with familiarity, that comes naturally. (Sharks
do not like the taste of Homo sap meat anyway. When
they see surfers, stuffed into black wet suits, lying on
surfboards with their feet in flippers, the sharks' poor
eyesight sometimes mistakes them for seals, which some
species of sharks do eat. They take a bite of a surfer and
then—like Count Dracula in Paul Morrisey's sixties film,
deceived into thinking that the Italian girl he sank his
fangs into is a virgin—puke it out when they realize
their mistake.) You feel your eyes and your big bloated
body completely exposed to that yellow eye which reveals nothing whatever of its response to you. Sharks
have skin like us, not scales, but no expression. No
tremors of curiosity, distrust, repugnance, antagonism, or
menace shiver or crease that skin. There is no cause for
fear. Under the gaze of the shark, your eyes entirely
cease to be organs for observing, cease to be organs, become only surfaces on your nonfunctional anorganic
plenum. Time extends in a motionless span, coming
from nowhere, going nowhere.

A tune is not launched by an advance representation
of the final note, and its evolution is nowise purposive.

Bestiality

In singing a tune, or in patterning our finger movements through our hair into a kinetic melody, we are also not controlled by another movement. Tunes do not imitate but answer refrains that start and stop in the streets, in the fields, and in the clouds.

Crickets in the meadows and cicadas in the trees, coyotes in the night hills, frogs in the ponds and whales in the oceans, birds and bats in the skies make our planet continually resound with chant. Humans do not begin to sing, and do not sing, in dead silence. Our voices begin to purr, hum, and crescendo in the concerto and cacophony of nature and machines.

J. M. G. Le Clézio was long puzzled by the particular features of the singing of the Lacandon Indians in Chiapas—a music of cries and noises, without melody or harmony, repetitious, night music made clandestinely and in solitude, a music made with a monophonic bamboo tube, a pipe with but two holes, a drum, a scraper, a shell, a bell, a music that does not seek to be beautiful, that is not addressed to anyone. Then, during long rainy season nights, Le Clézio heard how their songs, leaving words and meaning behind, pick up and join the basso continuo of the frogs, the dogs, the spider-monkeys, the agoutis, the wild boars, and the sloths in the tropical night.

Insects sing with their torsos, their legs, and their wings; human animals sing with their throats, their chests, their torsos, their legs, and their fingers. Human animals sing with the terrestrial, oceanic, and celestial animals, and with the reeds and the ant-hollowed branches of didgeridoos, the catgut strings and the drum-hides, the brass and the bronze. Around the campfires of hunter-gatherers from time immemorial, humans have sung with their bodies, the dances of the Maasai composing visual melodies against the staves of elephant grass, people in the slums of Salvador in Brazil sauntering the samba, with the pulsating movements of the cats and dogs of the alleys, into the staves the cars are drawing. In the imposed silence of university libraries, the bodies of students are bent over books, but how much of their bodies sing—their ant-antennae feet rhythmically tapping the floor, their hummingbird fingers dancing elegant melodies in their hair.

The parents of a first baby feel all sorts of feelings about that baby—astonishment, curiosity, pride, tenderness, the pleasure of caring for a new life, the mother's resentment of the father's inability to share the tedium of nursing and his unwillingness to share the changing of diapers, and the father's jealousy as the woman he so recently chose to devote himself to exclusively, as she him, now pours most of her affection on the baby. What does the baby feel, aside from hunger and discomfort? Whatever feelings simmer in that opaque and unfocused body are blurred and nebulous. Brought up in a state orphanage, the child would reach the age to be transferred to the automobile or tobacco factory assembly line with still opaque and blurred feelings. Brought up in a high-rise apartment where the parents stay home weeknights watching action movies on television while fondling their gun collection and go for rides weekends through a landscape of streets, boulevards, underpasses, and highways, seeing only other cars outside the window, the child would reach sexual maturity with the feelings of Ballard and Vaughan in J. G. Ballard's *Crash*.

Is it not animal emotions that make our feelings intelligible? Human emotions are interlaced with practical, rational, utilitarian calculations that tend to neutralize them—to the point that the human parent, finding her time with the baby dosed out between personal and career interests, may no longer know if she feels something like parental love, not knowing how much of her concern for her child is concern with her own image or her representative. It is when we see the parent bird attacking the

Bestiality

cat, the mother elephant carrying her dead calf in grief for three days, that we believe in the reality of maternal love. So much of the human courage we see celebrated is inseparable from peer pressure and the craving for celebrity, even the possibility of profit. It is the bull in the corrida that convinces us of the natural reality of fearlessness.

Is not the force of our emotions that of the other animals? Human infants are tedious at table, picking at their food, playing with it, distracted from it; they pick up voracity from the puppy absorbed with total Zen attentiveness at his dish. They come to feel curiosity with a white mouse poking about the papers and ballpoints on their father's desk. Their first heavy toddling shifts into tripping with the robins hopping across the lawn. They come to feel buoyancy in the midst of the park pigeons shifting so effortlessly from ground to layers of sundrenched air. They come to feel sullenness when they try to pet the arthritic old dog the retired cop is walking in the park. They contract righteousness and indignation from the mother hen suddenly ruffled up and stabbing with her beak when they try to remove a chick. They pick up feelings of smoldering wrath from the snarling chained dog in the neighbor's yard and they try out those feelings by snarling when they are put under restraints or confined. Temper in a human infant dies away of itself; it is from finding reverberating in himself the howling of dogs locked up for the night, the bellowing of tigers, the fury of bluebirds pursuing hawks in the sky, that his rage extends to nocturnal, terrestrial, and celestial dimensions. If an infant brought up in a highrise apartment, where all the paths he walks outside are paved and even dogs and cats are forbidden, still acquires feelings other than those which purring, growling, or roaring machines transmit to him, it is because he has contact with humans who have made contact with the living forces of nature.

Bestiality

The curled fingers of an infant ease into tenderness in holding the kitten but not tight, and rumble into contentment from stroking the kitten's fur with the pressure and rhythm that set it purring. Though the parrot can clutch with a vise-grip around a perch while sleeping, he relaxes his claws on the arm of an infant and never bites the ear he affectionately nibbles, extending his neck and spreading his wings to be caressed in all the softness of his down feathers; with him the infant discovers that her hands are not just retractile hooks for grabbing, but organs to give pleasure. In contact with the puppy mouthing and licking his legs and fingers and face, the infant discovers his lips are not just fleshy traps to hold in the food and his tongue not just a lever to shift it into his throat, but organs that give, give pleasure, give the pleasures of being kissed. Feeling the lamb extending its belly and its thighs and raising its tail for stroking, the infant discovers that her hands, her thighs, and her belly are organs to give pleasure.

Far from the human libido naturally destining us to a member of our species and of the opposite sex, when anyone who has not had intercourse with the other animals, has not felt the contented cluckings of a hen stroked on the neck and under the wings rumbling through his own flesh, has not kissed a calf's mouth raised to her own, has not mounted the smooth warm flanks of a horse, has not been aroused by the powdery feathers of cockatoos and the ardent chants of insects in the summer night, lies with a member of his or her own species, she and he are only consummating tension release, getting their rocks off. When we, in our so pregnant expression, *make love* with someone of our own species, we also make love with the horse and the dolphin, the kitten and the macaw, the powdery moths and the lustful crickets.

As our bodies become orgasmic, our posture, held oriented for tasks, collapses; the diagrams for manipulations

and operations dissolve from our legs and hands, which
roll about as though dismembered, exposed to the touch
and tongue of another, moved by another. Our lips
loosen, soften, glisten with saliva, lose the train of sentences; our throats issue babble, giggling, moans, and
sighs. Our sense of ourselves, our self-respect shaped in
fulfilling a function in the machinic and social environment, our dignity maintained in multiple confrontations,
collaborations, and demands, dissolve; the ego loses its
focus as center of evaluations, decisions, and initiatives.
Our impulses, our passions, are returned to animal irre-
sponsibility. The sighs and moans of another that pulse
through our nervous excitability, the spasms of pleasure
and torment in contact with the nonprehensile surfaces
of our bodies, our cheeks, our bellies, our thighs, irradi-
ate across the substance of our sensitive and vulnerable
nakedness. The lion and stallion mane, the hairy bull
chest, the hairy monkey armpits, the feline pelt of the
mons veneris, the hairy satyr anus, exert a vertiginous attraction. We feel feline and wolfish, foxy and bitchy; the
purrings of kittens reverberate in our orgasmic strokings,
our squirrelly fingers race up and down the trunk and
limbs of another, our clam vagina opens, our erect cobra-
head penis snakes its way in. Our muscular and vertebrate bodies transubstantiate into ooze, slime, mammalian sweat, and reptilian secretions, into minute
tadpoles and releases of hot moist breath nourishing the
floating microorganisms of the night air.

Human sexuality is not just what priggish suburban-
ites call animal sex, the random and mindless copulation
of their domestic dogs; it elaborates all the refinements
of eroticism. Lust enlists all the Platonic eros which
craves the beauty that looks immortal and the immortality of beauty; it elaborates the skills and the arts of seduction, the teasing and provocative usage of language,
metaphor and metonymy, synecdoche and irony, the no

that is a yes and the yes that is a no, the specific pleasure in appearance, simulacra, and masquerade, the challenge and purely imaginary stakes of games.

In this the courtesan specialized in the rites of eroticism is in symbiosis with the resplendent quetzal whose extravagantly arrayed, glittering plumage serves no utilitarian function; the cavalry officer is in symbiosis with the coral fish whose Escher designs do not outline the functional parts and organs of their bodies and whose fauvist colors are no more camouflage than are the officer's white jodhpurs and scarlet cape. The ceremonies and etiquette with which courtship was elaborated in the palaces of the Sun King were not more ritualized than the courtship of Emperor penguins in Antarctica, the codes of chivalry in medieval Provence not more idealized than the spring rituals of impalas in the East African savannah, the rites of seduction of geishas in old Kyoto not more refined than those of black-neck cranes in moonlit marshes.

Humans have from earliest times made themselves erotically alluring by grafting upon themselves the splendors of the other animals, the filmy plumes of ostriches, the secret luster of mother-of-pearl oysters, the springtime gleam of fox fur. Until the gardens of Versailles, perfumes were made not with the nectar of flowers but with the musks of rodents. The days-long songs of whales and the dance floors cleared of vegetation and decorated with shells and flowers that birds of paradise make for their intoxicated dances exhibit the extravagant erotic elaborations far beyond reproductive copulation in which humans have joined with the other animals.

Today, in our Internet world where everything is reduced to digitally coded messages, images, and simulacra instantaneously transmitted from one human to another, it is in our passions for the other animals that we learn all the rites and sorceries, the torrid and teasing presence, and the ceremonious delays, of eroticism.

3

Faces

Chimpanzees, gorillas, Neanderthals, Cro-Magnons are
moving with the sun crossing the sky, moving with the
wind rustling the leaves of baobabs and acacias, the
movements of their legs and hands syncopating with the
bends and springs of the elephant grass. A flight of
flamingos draws their heads skyward, a rush of wilde-
beests drives wildness into them, they do a punk slam-
dance with the scavenger hyenas. Their hands are extended upon one another's arms, backs, legs, heads,
moving with the tensions and flexions of torsos. They lie
on the ground, shifting under the recoil of the grass and
the stirring of small insects; overhead the branches laden
with leaves and berries sway with the gusts of wind.
Their fingers are clasping the fingers of those leafy
branches, berries falling from fingers to fingers. Their
fingers are replying to the movements of their lips and
tongues, also bringing berries to and taking berries from
one another's fingers and lips. Inside their mouths
marshes of bacteria pulsate, neutralizing the toxins in
those berries.

They murmur with the rustling leaves, answer the
chatter of vervets and mandrills, the bellowings of ele-
phants, and the cries of shrikes and eagles. They hum
and chant with one another as they move. Outbursts of
laughter spread among them. In laughter they recognize
one another as members of the same species and are attracted to one another. They wail and weep together over
a lifeless child, over an adult dead of fever. They intone
blessings over exquisite forest-floor and grandiose cosmic

Faces

events that delight them; they utter curses that challenge
and pursue evil forces to their redoubts. Their pleasures
 and afflictions are not inner subjective states; they are radiations. The laughing, grieving, blessing, and cursing
gestures and words with which they hold on to things
and events are not signs designating meanings fixed in a
code.

As the sun descends and the darkness softens the hard
edges of things, their eyelids close. Lying on the ground,
they rest their heads on one another's bellies and thighs,
their legs and hands extending and retracting when the
torsos they rest on shift to open bends of intestines for
cascading leaves and berries and four hundred species of
gluttonous bacteria. Through the long night the wind
stirs, the leaves of grass hum as they shift positions.

The feet of one human animal stumble on the cliff
face; the hand of the other grasps and pulls him erect.
Gradations of strength are established in assisting and in
contending with one another. Among gregarious animals, contention involves assistance, and becomes contests to establish leadership. The spiral horns of two
buck kudus lower, swerve, lock; their legs push; the one
buckles and falls. The lead kudu, sighting a lion, paws
the ground, the calf's tail swirls and its legs spring and
sprint. One human, the alpha male, drives off the cupidinous junior male, who feints, and another cupidinous son
runs off with the alpha female. The male or female
human with the most experience and endurance leads
the pack, watching for danger.

Then, in the desert, in the steppes, there arose the
despot. He no longer wrestled with the others in the
alpha male position, exposing his moves to adversary
forces and charges, exposing his legs to be kicked under
him, putting himself in the front line before dangers to
the group. The despot covered his head with a blank

Faces

screen, his face. On this blank screen signs take form.[1]
The equivocal laughters and wanton gropings of the
multitude run up against his face as against a blank wall.

A face faces to express meanings. A face faces to express subjective feelings. More than "express"—there
are no meanings without a blank wall on which signs are
inscribed and effaced; there is no self-conscious consciousness without black holes where its states of pleasure and displeasure turn.

The surfaces of the animal heads of the multitude
are animated with the movements of the body and of
the surrounding things. These heads shiver with the cold
wind, giggle with the tickling seaweed, glow in the monsoon, grimace with the weight of the rock the hands
grip, quake in the night, laugh and weep and yawn by
contagion. The words of the multitude, leading their
eyes, their laughter, and their grief upon things and
events are resonant with overtones and polydirectional.
They are equivocal; there is no laughter without tears, no
blessing without curses.

A face is a field that accepts some expressions and
connections and neutralizes others. It is a screen and a
framework. To be confronted with a face is to envision a
certain range of things that could be expressed on it and
to have available a certain range of things one could address to it. One sees what one might say, what one should
not have said.

The pronouncements of the despot extend in linear
progression to align the crisscrossing sounds, tones, and
also movements coming from the multitude. In his
words, one meaning, one direction, is fixed. The words
the despot utters are directives, imperatives.

When a question "What is there?" arose in the multitude, the words that responded led them to see or to in-———
voke the thing or event itself. Now, faced with the words

Faces

of the despot, they must ask: "What did he mean?" His words separate a meaning from the pattern, directions, and force of things and events. Their words must capture his meaning; his meaning is designated by repeatable words. His words are signs, repeatably designating one and the same fixed meaning.

The laughter, weeping, blessing, and cursing of the multitude are fields of force and radiation, not inner states of self-consciousness. On the blank wall of the face of the despot, there are black holes dark as night in which his eyes and his ears are suspended. The words of his subjects facing him—aligning their actions upon him—enter these black holes, where his pleasure and displeasure simmer. A spiral of subjectivity turns in these black holes: a movement turning on itself and existing for itself. There the sound and fury of the multitude are directed to a pleasure and displeasure that turns on itself and sanctions and blames.

The authority of the despot is the black holes of his face. To be faced by him is to be judged. His look aligns the laughing and lustful advances, rhythms, and divagations in the multiplicity, directs them to himself, where they are sanctioned or terminated in the black holes of his look. The multitude will know his pleasure and his displeasure only in words put on the blank wall of his face. His arbitration operates by binary oppositions, dichotomies and bipolarities: No. Yes.

The despot demands that his subjects give an account of themselves. They must account for what they did, what they will do. They must inwardly code what they are now as coherent with, consequent upon, what they did yesterday. They must make what they will do tomorrow be the consequence of what they say today. Their movements must no longer be immediate responses to the rhythms and rushes about them. Their voices no

Faces

longer resonate, chant, invoke, call forth; they respond to
the voice of a law that orders one to move on down the
line. Before the despot they extend over their heads the
blank surfaces of faces. They are these blank walls for
signs—nothing but subjects of discourse, coding, order-
ing their animal bodies.

The despot orders his subjects to exercise surveillance
over their movements. They themselves are to make the
present movement validate the past movement, and
make the present moment a pledge for the movement to
come. They are to line up the movements of their animal bodies before the black holes of their own looks,
where these movements are subjected to judgment, to
yes and to no.

About the wandering multitude the environment
streams by. They move with its patterns, directions, and
forces. About the despot who stands facing them, the tur-
bulent prairies, winds, and desert become a landscape.
The pulsings, shiftings, fluxes, and thrusts of continental
shelves, oceans and skies, the other animals, the plants
and the viruses are covered over with meanings sanctioned in his pleasure and displeasure. Drifting dunes
and shifting shadows become a face of the earth inscribed with signs. In the black holes of its glades and
caverns, its forbidden sanctuaries, he sees ancestral and
demonic passions addressed to his subjectivity.

The polis, the geopolitical empire: in every cubicle of
the high-rises, the blank screen of a television set faces
the inmates. The blank screen flickers—lines appear
within an oval, angular, or round border: the prime minister, the minister of defense, the leader of the opposing
army, the president of the Chamber of Commerce, the
president of Quantas, the star of the national rugby
team, the star of the Hollywood superproduction face
millions of viewers. The lines, wrinkles, traits of the face

Faces

oscillate. One does not see, divine, or touch the nervous circuitry, the thin strands of muscles, and the inner rivers coursing billions of enzymes, bacteria, and macrophages in a depth behind this blank wall; the face is all surface, a signboard on which a succession of words will appear. In ninety-second sound bites words will fix a meaning for all the wobbling, swarming lines of sallies and feints in the electoral campaign, in the economy, in the stadiums, in the new fashions, in the new trend in pop singers. The blank wall of the face is perforated with black holes; in them the eyes turn, sanctioning or censuring, yes, no. The president, the minister of the interior, the leader of the opposing army, the president of the multinational corporation, the captain of the Olympics team, the heavy metal star is authoritatively pleased, is authoritatively displeased.

In the streets and corridors, in the offices and factories, schools and hospitals, legs move toward goals fixed by words. Lest they stray, there are words written at highway intersections, at street corners, on doors, and along the corridors of shopping malls. Hands reach toward words written on boxes, bottles, and cans. Fingers touch letters and words on security alarm pads, microwaves, phonographs, television sets, computers, and cellular phones. The posture in the torso and neck responds to words—attention: the boss is looking; the highway cop is checking the radar screen; the father, teacher, tour guide is looking over there; the judge, foreman, council member, coach, star has arrived; the face is appearing on the screen. Attention. At ease. Attention. At ease.

The citizens do not lean against, entwine, fondle, and smell one another's bodies, feeling the streams and cascades and backwaters pulsing within; they deal with the blank walls of faces extended over their own heads. They have to face one another and question one another.

Faces

A question is not a supplication, an entreaty, nor a velleity for knowledge just put out in the air; it is already an order, a command. (Beggars, the destitute, pupils, factory workers, enlisted soldiers, prisoners, and patients have no right to question; they can only entreat.[2]) A question commands a certain focus of attention, a selection of resources on hand, a certain type of language. It lays down a direction; it imposes a directive to think further down a certain track.

Facing one another, we require responsibility. And responsibility requires integrity—not only sincerity but also an integration of the faculties and resources of the speaker. One has not only to respond to the greetings and questions of others, but also to answer for what one says and said five minutes ago and yesterday and last year. "But you said. . . ." "But you promised. . . ." To say "I" is not simply to designate oneself as the one now making this utterance; it is to reiterate the same term and attribute to it again utterances and deeds previously predicated of it. If we have changed, we have to reinstate what we were by way of offering a motive for what we have now become. "Yes I promised to get a job and get off welfare, but I was injured in the bus collision."

To find our identity in facing others is to exist and act under accusation. It is to have to provide a coherent verbal justification for movements that emanate from our body. We cultivate a memory in which everything is filed in an accessible system; we make what we feel and do today consistent with what we felt and did yesterday, what we were trained to do, what we were brought up to be. Know thyself! The unexamined life is not worth living! What we think and say today is a pledge and a commitment, to which tomorrow, next year, the next decade are subjugated. The blank wall and black holes of the face of Socrates lurk about in the workshops, assembly

Faces

halls, and studios of the city, accusing and discrediting the carpenter, the leader of men or of women, who cannot give a linear rational justification for his or her actions—discrediting even the artist, the poet, the composer who cannot give a verbal explanation of his or her composition.

The temptation not to answer for something that was seen or said or done through our organism yesterday—to attribute it to another psychic agency, and to begin to break up into discontinuous psychic sequences—is the very formula for antisocial existence. The schizophrenic is a sociopath. Multiple personality disorder is the final psychosis psychiatry has to deal with. Society sees the sociopath not simply in the violent—violence can be, as in policemen or professional boxers, perfectly socialized—but in someone who leads a double or triple life.

The face extends down the whole length of a body. The hands and fingers no longer probe, punch, and caress with the furry caterpillars, the raccoons, and the octopods; held at a distance from contact with any other body, they gesticulate, diagraming meaningful signals and punctuations consistent with the words set forth. The very genitals, exposed in the collapse of posture and skills, the collapse of will, the dissolute decomposition of orgasm undergoing material transubstantiations, solidifying, gelatinizing, liquefying, vaporizing, are under accusation the whole length of their existence: They must mean something; they must carry the dead weight of a meaning; they must express respect for the person, the ego, the identity, the authority of the face; they must confirm the partner's identity; they must serve the population policy of the nation-state and its patron god. Everything animal in the body must be covered up, with clothing that extends the face—the blank surfaces of the business suit and the tailored two-piece suit of the career

Faces

woman with the black holes of its buttons, the blue of deliveryman's uniform and the white of painter's dungarees, the uniform of fight attendant and politician's wife and university student, uniforms on which orders are seen and where black holes of subjectivity judge and sanction. The surfaces of clothing accept some expressions and connections and neutralize others. The blank wall of a face, extended over a body, detaches the body's skin from its pulsations, flexions, and exudations and makes it a surface for the display of meaning.

But it also happens that the depth of the body invades the face, darkening it with ambiguity and ardor. The expressive lines of the lips and cheeks vacillate, lose the train of the expression they were formulating. They shimmer with the caresses of the sunlight, tremble with the throbbing of the insects and rustling trees. Into the smooth contours of the cheeks, blank for the inscription of signals, there emerges an exposed and susceptible carnality. From behind the carapace of clothing, all the animals within migrate to the face, sole surface of exposure, to connect with the animals outside. The lips crave contact with the lips of the dolphin, the nose brushes the whiskered nose of the Siamese cat, the cheeks seek the caresses of ferns in the forest night.

When our gaze meets such a face, we see freckles that stream off in the autumn leaves, eyes we cross over instead of seeing ourselves in them, looks where our looks can surf. We see the mane of the centaur-woman billowing across the windy prairie, sunlight dancing across the wrinkles of the old woman feeding pigeons in the park, sand dunes of the cheeks and lips of a woman in Hiroshi Teshigehara's film *Woman of the Dunes*, gelatinous crystals of the eyes in which we see the effulgence of stars that burned out millions of light-years ago, open mouth

Faces

into which we push our tongue upon gardens of six hundred species of microorganisms.

When someone's greeting trembles with the dance of springtime or threnody of winter, his voice invites us to hear the murmur of nature that resounds in it. When another turns her eyes to us, she does not look in our eyes only to order them or to find the map of the landscape; her eyes seek out first the vivacity and delight of the light in our eyes which summon her forth. The gaze of another that touches us lightly and turns aside, and invokes not the glare of our gaze but the darkness our eyes harbor, refracts to us the summons of the impersonal night.

Beneath the face as a surface for signs, we see the skin in its carnality and vulnerability. We see in the spasms, the wrinkles, the wounds on her skin, the urgency of her hunger, her thirst, her cold, her fever, her fear, or her despair. We are immediately afflicted with these wounds, these wants, this suffering. In our hands extended to clasp her hands, touch turns to tact and tenderness.

The suffering we see may well be a suffering that does not seek to be consoled: let us beware of setting out to alleviate a suffering that another needs and clings to as his or her destiny—the inner torments of Beethoven, the hardships and heartaches of the youth who has gone to join the guerrillas in the mountains, the grief of the mother mourning the loss of her child. To be afflicted with another's suffering requires that we care about the things the sufferer cares for. The suffering we see in the bloodless white of an anguished face may well be not the suffering of her own hunger and thirst, but suffering for the animals in her care that are dying of the drought or for the peregrines in the poisoned skies, for the crumbling temple, for the nests of seabirds drowned in the tidal wave, for the glaciers melting under skies whose carbon-dioxide layers are trapping the heat of the earth.

Faces

And is there not always joy in the face before us, even joy in suffering? In the midst of grief and torment there is an upsurge of force that affirms the importance and truth of what one is tormented by, of what one grieves over. This upsurge of force that affirms itself unrestrictedly is joy—joy at having known what is now lost, and joy in finding us.

The thumbs-up from the Brazilian street kid—his mouth voraciously gobbling our extra spaghetti, too full to smile or say *obrigado*—is not only contentment in the satisfaction of his hunger; it is the joy of being in the streets so full of excitements and in the glory of the sun reigning over the beaches of Rio. His laughter pealing over the squalls and blasts of the urban jungle gives rise to his hunger and to his relishing the goodness of restaurant spaghetti.

4

The Religion
of Animals

In the city people are moving down sidewalks, up and
down escalators, along aisles; they are stationed in the
driver's seat of buses, at gas pumps, computers, and cash
registers. There is a low-intensity fear in them. They
avoid turning in certain directions, flailing their arms or
poking their hands in certain ways. They respect invisible barriers.

Among people constrained by invisible cordons, ropes,
fences, and gates, we feel safe, free to attend to our needs
and concerns. We feel that the bulk and mass of our bodies present such barriers to them. As though afraid of us,
they avoid colliding with us or entangling their limbs in
ours. We feel safe in our workplace when others treat us
with respect, considerateness, and tact.

Perceiving those invisible barriers, corridors, and
gates continually gives rise to judgments—judgments
that this one, that one, these people or those are or are
not acting in the right way. That motorcycle missed us
by inches. Those people are queuing along the building,
leaving space on the sidewalk for others to get by. Those
people are blaring their hi-fi all afternoon. And we see
moralizing judgments in the stern glance directed our
way when we zigzag through the room full of people, the
knitting of the brow when we talk too loud, the ostentatious turning away when we sit on the bus seat in our
sweat-dank clothes.

This moralizing perception gives rise to a second, rationalizing perception. Seeing where those walking or

running legs are heading, what these arms are reaching for, brings to flush a further system of corridors, channels, and railings. Those people are queuing along the building in order to get tickets for the bullfight. That woman pushing and shoving through the crowd will not make the plane anyway. Perceiving the reasons for the movements of the people about us is perceiving the destinations, the targets, as well as the obstacles and pitfalls in their way.

The moralizing perception does not depend on this rationalizing perception. Out in the street we rarely look to see what the workers in construction sites or those glimpsed behind windows bent over machines or people alone on park benches are doing and why. We only scan the scene to see that there are no locks broken, no fences being pushed over, no turnstiles being uprooted.

Catching sight of the goals of people's movements, the purposes of their maneuvers, gives us a sharper sense of the ways clear for us. The two cars ahead have their turn signals flashing, so that street is one-way the right way. The running steps behind us in the dark are just those of a jogger. We feel an additional degree of assurance when we sense that the goals of our movements, the purposes of our operations, the reasons for our moves are visible to those about us.

When, in response to our question, others tell us what they are doing and why, they formulate what they have to say in terms that make sense to us. When we do not bother to ask, it is because we suppose the explanations they give to others would make sense to us. The invisible guardrails and turnstiles we perceive in their advance and the channels and partition walls we perceive about their operations make us think that their explanations would make sense to anyone.

We see that they are constrained to do only what they can justify to others. This evidence of everyone held to be responsible, living under accusation, justifies our moralizing perceptions.

Our eyes are drawn to exemplary individuals. We are grateful for those who do what is right, even at cost to themselves. We perceive an inner force of conviction that prevents them from doing the wrong thing even if they would profit or obtain immediate gratification from doing it. We find assurance in the honest clerk at the cash register who returns the right change, including the extra ten-dollar bill we handed her. We even find assurance in the adolescent who pauses a moment to hold the door for us while his companions saunter on.

We perceive also an inner force of principle in some individuals that drives them to prevent wrongdoing, even at the risk of disadvantage, injury, or death to themselves. We count on such rectitude in the uniformed police, but we know that even they are ineffective unless a percentage of citizens is willing to risk harm to themselves to report crimes and inform on suspects. Our trust in the moral community rests on the assurance that there is that quantum of fortitude in the bus driver who will take responsibility for the security of the passengers, in the shoppers in the store who would protect an old or infirm person from a purse-snatcher.

Yet we are also drawn to people who are not exemplary, who do not illustrate good sense and responsibility, who are temperamental as stallions, mercurial as falcons, sensual as cheetahs. Before them we relax our compulsion to judge, no longer feel that they have a responsibility to answer to and for what they do and say. We are enthralled by the human animal, the animality in humans, the traits humans acquire in symbiosis with noble animals.

The paleolithic cave paintings of Cosquer, Chauvet, and Lascaux demonstrate that the most ancient gods of humanity were other animals, perceived by hunter-gatherers as not bound by taboos, more sacred and more demonic than humans. They were the noble animals—tigers, lions, jaguars, eagles, condors, cobras, animals of courage. The caves of Lascaux contain but one depiction of a human—a stick figure with the head of a bird; the Cosquer cave contains one figure of a crudely drawn genderless human; the Chauvet cave has one figure of a bison whose lower body is that of a human. In Les Trois Frères caves there is a figure with antlers, owl eyes, a horse's tail, wolf ears, bear paws, and human feet and penis. Who isn't struck by the images and carvings of lion-headed humans, figures half-human-half-bull, figures half-human-half-stag, human with the head of a fox or an ibis or a cat in the ancient art of Egypt, Mesopotamia, Southeast Asia, and America? From other species—the lions of Assyria, the cobras of Vedic India, the birds of paradise of the Papuans, the jaguars of the Mayas, and the condors of the Inca—nobility came and comes to the human species.

The noble impulses are nowise contrived to serve human needs and wants, human whinings. The impulses and the external appearance of the noble animals lend themselves to the utilitarian explanations of biologists. But when a human animal comes to inhabit other animals' territory with them, or even inhabit their bodies as they his, the movements released by the excess energies in his body are composed with the differentials, directions, rhythms, and speeds of their bodies. The human body thereby acquires movements that are not acquisitive, stabilizing, nor productive. The woman who rides a stallion lurches with the surges of its impulses, feeling the thrill of speed and the decompression of retardation. While the speed of the stallion serves the animal in the wild, the thrill of riding nowise serves the woman in the corridors, cubicles, and desks of the rationalized human community. Biologists will explain the immediate urge to attack in the bull as protective of his harem and of his own more vigorous genes, but the fearlessness that the torero picks up from the bull no longer has this biological finality and becomes bravado.

The curve of a cheek, breast, or torso, the robust harmony of the salient muscles, the richness of a complexion, the splendor of a mane of hair draw our eyes irresistibly, on policewomen as on idlers, on the streetkid knifed and being laid on a stretcher as on the paramedics themselves. We cannot stop dreaming of them. When someone of spectacular physical beauty appears, in the airport, in the restaurant, in the office, this apparition nowise fits in. It is nowise justified by the moralizing and rationalizing perception we have of the people at their posts and moving down invisible corridors. And these latter now appear somehow vulgar and mean.

From Socrates—whose physical ugliness Nietzsche noted and made much of—to John Rawls, our ethics has not known what to make of physical splendor. It has not given the name of virtue to the compulsion of a man to acquire the strong and proportioned musculature of the elk, the compulsion of a woman to move with the grace of a panther. This compulsion does not derive from ethical culture but arises on invitation from nature, whose primal drive for beauty arrays such a carnival parade of coral fish, butterflies, and birds, and decorates the shells of blind mollusks with designs and colors as splendid as those of pheasants. The drive creative of beauty is so fundamental in nature that all our interest in nature is a marvel at her beauty. We marvel at someone of our species because we catch sight of the sunfish or the dragonfly, the leopard or the eagle in them.

Beyond our trained adaptive energies, we long for gratuitous animal vigor, visible in the bounding of antelopes across the fields, otters across the rapids. We see it in the laborers who, after a full day of grueling toil, run off in boisterous horseplay. While the electric storm pounds the stranded cars and flooded streets of Rio, from our hotel window we watch the stormy beach below, where, strobe-lit by lightning, teams of Brazilians shout hits and misses in a game of beach volleyball.

There is a health beyond health, triumphant in the quantity of onslaughts, contagions, and corruptions it passes through, admits into itself, and overcomes. Such is the health of sharks and condors. Such is the preposterous health of the young woman come back from trekking the length of Tibet, the brazen health of the young couple who climbed onto bicycles at the Arctic Ocean and now, a year later, we meet in Tierra del Fuego.

There is also an animal vigor of the mind that seduces us. We find assurance and pleasure in witnessing the competence, the mastery of the details, and the calm working out of a solution by a police officer, a doctor, and a government administrator. But there is a kind of mind that fascinates us even when it is running on idle. Such is the mind that contemplates depravities without flinching, without being contaminated, that, like a flock of starlings or seagulls chattering and clattering over garbage dumped in ravines or in the sea, rises above with banter, wisecracks, and laughter. We see this health of mind in the cop who grew up in the neighborhood and knows all the schemes and scams, betrayals and self-deceits of the local punks, junkies, dealers, petty and major racketeers, but still enjoys no one's company more than theirs in their disreputable bars and hangouts. We love this health of mind in the whorehouse madam who has seen everything, believes nothing and no one, and still has a heart of gold and the good sense that the social workers and psychotherapists into whose hands her cronies fall from time to time do not have. We see it in the father who can't help laughing over his son's mockery of his paternalism, in the young executive who can't help laughing when a junkie jeers at his BMW, that car designed by the same nerd who designed the briefcase, in the cop who finds himself squirming in laughter over the inventive insults he gets from the streetwalker he is arresting.

Youth beguiles us as maturity never does or can. Youth is insolent, impetuous, brash. Without cocky impulsiveness, youth is merely impotence. And how we are delighted by the shameless old woman who spent her widowhood indulging every whim and pleasure, and when she dies the family attorney discovers that she has just spent the last franc of her husband's savings and investments!

Socrates, who claimed none of the intellectual or moral virtues, at his trial reminded his judges of his courage, of which they all were aware, proved three times in battle. Aristotle made courage the first virtue, for without courage, neither truthfulness nor magnanimity nor friendship nor even wit in conversation are possible. But Socrates erred in then setting out to formulate the ideas and beliefs—his arguments for immortality—

that would make courage possible. For courage, as the word indicates, is the force of the heart (*cor, cuer, coeur*) and sociological studies show that the same number of people die bravely and die cowardly among those who think that their death is the gateway to eternal bliss as among those who think their death is only annihilation. Shall we then say that courage rises up in us from our animal nature? But the courage of the torero rises in his confrontation with that of the black bull who charges into pain and death; the bravery of the diver becomes gallantry in his duel with the attacking damselfish, a creature that is but a few grams of jellied matter in seawater; the valor of the pilot of the Cessna rises fraternally with that of the albatross soaring and swooping through gale winds in mid-ocean.

In moving among other people, keeping sight of the corridors, gates, and turnstiles that constrain them, we are reassured by those in whom power and direction are consolidated. Years after their downfall, even tyrants such as Somoza, Marcos, and Pinochet are still revered by a third of the populace. We are reassured by every David who stands before a Goliath, whether his stone fells or misses him. But beyond the courage that defies, provokes, and challenges death, counting on the power we have, there is the blazing glory of the bravado that exposes itself needlessly to the unforgiving strokes of fate, the fatalities of chance.

There are games in which what one loses, if one loses, is completely disproportionate to what one wins, if one wins. One stands to lose everything. Is it not the intrinsic glory of bravado that accounts for the fact that we feel a kind of indifference and even disdain for someone who has never lied, never cheated on a lover, never duped or taken advantage of a friend, never got drunk, never

thrown away a fistful of hard-earned money, never
played the fool by loving someone who was only toying
with him or her?

We watch fascinated a helicopter rescue operation, a
mountaineer scaling a vertical cliff, a duet of martial
artists performing actions intricate, skillful, and effective. But nothing so mesmerizes us as erotic activities. A
woman bursting with erotic pride and decorated with
brazen ostentation, pumping her way down the corridor
of a hospital, draws our eyes away from the meritorious
and medically effective activities of the nurses and doctors. Our late capitalist civilization is not alone in
shamelessly pursuing a double standard, honoring on
the one hand with medals, parades, and statues women
who have selflessly waged superhuman struggles to save
their children from hard times or crack gangsters, who
have saved the neighborhood from developers and the
environment from nuclear pollutants, and on the other
hand honoring with jewels and legends cabaret perform-
ers, vixens over whom diplomats and heads of state have
lost their heads, Carmens whose fickle hearts could not
sustain a love more than six weeks and for whom an
endless succession of men have left their wives and children. Nothing a male does—a window-washer working
in the wind sixty floors over the street, a fireman climbing a ladder to rescue an invalid from a blazing building,
a champion boxing with elegance as well as power—so
fevers the mind as a male flaunting all his virile voluptuousness. The corrida, where the bullfighter's supple
slender body is poised like a dancer's, his genitals
flaunted in jeweled splendor in his skin-tight garb,
provocatively exposed to the horn of the black bull, is
the supreme theater for the glorification of virility in
erotic bravado.

The Religion of Animals

We naked apes have become erotically seductive to one another by acquiring the splendor of lion and stallion manes in our hair, exposing the luster of mollusks in our eyes, adopting the grace of egrets and plovers in our biped strolling and sauntering, revealing the sleekness of eels and fish in our nakedness. The gratuity, the bravado, the heedless expenditures in our pursuit of the demonic grail of a flashing grin, a satiny breast, a proud erection, are traits that we have acquired in our romance with foxes and leopards courting and competing with tooth and nail, with pheasants spraying across the grass their glittering plumes, and with ocean mollusks exposing their nacreous colors and forms to devotees and to predators.

The male emperor penguins huddle on the ice shelf under raging blizzards for nine months of the Antarctic winter, all their metabolic processes devoted to keeping warm in temperatures of minus-seventy degrees Fahrenheit the eggs that the female emperor penguins have given over to their care. When the eggs hatch, they nourish the chicks with the secretions of their throats until the winter breaks and the females can return with krill from the open seas. House wrens in Pennsylvania gardens hurl themselves shrieking into the eyes of cats that are climbing to their nests. The stingers of bees are barbed, and the bee can detach itself from the enemy it stings only by fatally tearing its own body: every bee that stings an importunate suburbanite gives its life for the life of the hive. The nonhuman animals give not merely of their surplus to the less fortunate; they give of the nourishing fluids of their own bodies; they give their very life. They do not seek prestige for gifts given freely. They do not imagine an infinite repayment beyond the death they give that others may live.

Our theoretical ethics from Aristotle to Marcel Mauss and Jacques Derrida finds intelligibility in gift-giving only by reinterpreting it in an economy of equivalent exchange, even if that means calculating prestige as recompense with interest. The impulse to give without calculation and without recompense, when it rises up compulsively in us, as it does every day, we have contracted in our commerce with animal nobility. How rarely do humans find the courage to say those fearful words "I love you"—fearful because we are never so vulnerable, never open to being so easily and so deeply hurt, as when we give ourselves over in love of someone! But from early infancy we have come to understand that instinct—in our kitten that so unreservedly gave itself over to its affection for us, in our cockatoo that in all her excitement upon seeing us wants nothing but to give us all her tenderness and high spirits.

How awesome the thirst for truth, when we contemplate it sovereign in the great scientist, the great explorer! Here is someone contemptuous of honors and wealth, craving a mind open to the most tragic realities, to the cosmic indifference of the universe to our wishes and to those of our species, craving to know with the wounds, rendings, and diseases of his or her own body the oceans and tundra, rain forest and glaciers. Human culture compensates with prizes and honor those who limit their curiosity and their research only to funded projects that will benefit the human species. It is not from human culture that those consumed with the thirst for truth learn to program their lives, but from the albatross that leaves its nest to sail all the latitudes of the planet and all its storms and icy nights for seven years before it touches earth again, in order to give its mature strength to raising offspring like itself. You, researchers and consolidators of knowledge, Nietzsche said, have only turned the ways of the universe into a spider web to trap your prey: that is because your soul does not fly like eagles over abysses.

How awesome the thirst for justice, when we contemplate it in a man like Gandhi, Che Guevara, or Nelson Mandela! They knew before they began that at the end of the path they were blazing lay ambush and extermination, or a life tortured from youth to old age in dungeons. Of the Sandinista guerrillas who made a blood pact to fight for the liberation of Nicaragua in 1962, only one, Tomás Borge, was not gunned down in the jungle, and he was captured and held in Somoza's prisons for years. After the Sandinista victory in 1979, Tomás Borge was selected by his comrades to be Minister of Interior. A few months later, his subordinates informed him that among the captured agents of Somoza's Guardia Nacional were the three men who had tortured him during the years of his incarceration. He went at once to the prison where they were held and ordered them to be brought before him. He looked intently at them, and verified that they were indeed his torturers. Then he ordered them to be liberated. No reasoning, reckoning, or calculation of how to manage one's life most profitably in human society has ever provided the motivation for the thirst for justice in which a human sacrifices his life—so often in vain!—and even less for the justice that liberates its enemies. "Justice, which began," Nietzsche wrote, "with 'everything is paid for, everything must be paid for,' ends by winking and letting those incapable of paying their debt go free: it ends, as does every good thing on earth, by overcoming itself. This self-overcoming of justice: one knows the beautiful name it has given itself—*mercy*." Nietzsche went on to say that the noblest and most courageous humans contract this justice that overcomes itself from their commerce with lions, who are always covered with ticks and flies seeking shelter and nourishment on them. The lion does not rage against them: "What are my parasites to me? . . . May they live and prosper: I am strong enough for that!"[1]

5

Blessings
and Curses

Born in a nourishing environment, a living organism
generates force in excess of what it needs to adjust to its
environment and compensate for its periodic lacks. It is
not agitated by hungers alone; it moves to discharge excess energies. A guppy eats twice a day, taking up ten
minutes of its time; the rest of the day its movements are
the scherzo of play. Perhaps one percent of the movements of a student bent over a book in the library relate
to turning the pages; his fingers are stroking his thighs,
playing with his hair, drumming; his legs, forgotten by
his studious mind, are throbbing on the disco floor they
found in the night under the table.

The sentience of a living organism is not kept awake
by anxiety on the lookout for food and dangers; it projects its own movies into the sustaining ecosystem and
sensible environment into which it was born. Our kitten
turns the living room into a set for slapstick and slam-
dancing. Relative to their bodies, the brains of dolphins
are of equal size to those of humans and of equal or even
greater complexity, and, like those of humans, those
huge brains use a third of the metabolism of the body to
run them. Racing so effortlessly through the seas, their
oceanic environment putting so few problems to them,
what dolphins are using these brains for is a question
psychophysiology is only now trying to address. Humans'
comprehension is manual, based on eye-hand coordina-
tion, and linguistic. Dolphins' cerebral production must
be completely unlike ours. Besides the, after all, minimal

problem-solving our average day entails, we use the greater part of our cerebral energies to attend to everybody else's business—Michael Jackson's and that of *Australopithecus ramidus*, what the chipmunks in the garden and the cheetahs in the Serengeti, the guppies in the fishtank and the cocooned fish in the Kalahari desert, the comets and the black holes in outer space, and the dolphins are up to. We use our cerebral energies to weave halos, nimbuses, specters, images from the past, and legends into the somnolent summer landscape; to generate epics, mythical and metaphysical worlds, theogonies, fictions, and nonsense. Most of what anyone says is daft; most of what humanity has written is fudge. Whence it is such a pleasure to be with people and talk, whence cultures spread their enchantments over the ages.

At the end of the workday, dinner finished and dishes washed, our body has energy yet to burn. In the suburbs, they say one needs to sleep, because one needs to work the next day, because one needs to pay the mortgage on this red brick suburban refuge, and they stupefy their organisms with that nonprescription soporific, television, and the middlebrow depressant, beer. But the instincts of animal vitality drive you to the disco, to dance to euphoric collapse. Or to add another plate to your barbells in the gym and work out till muscle exhaustion on each set. To get all the energy back, nothing is easier: do nothing at all, have a good night's sleep, and the next time you come to the gym, you will find yourself adding yet another weight. You do not husband your mental resources for the morrow; you push your mind into the most difficult mathematical or metaphysical problem you know, until it is overcome with exhaustion. The next morning you wake up to find your mind yet more agile

and penetrating. At the end of the workday, you find
your cerebral circuitry buzzing with all the nonsense it
generated all day in excess of the attention it gave to the
assembly-line and the foreman's orders. You call up a
coworker to release in laughter the burlesque your brain
made out of the confrontation with the boss. One night
you call up everybody you know and tell all the jokes you
know, so that you will not be able to tell any of them
again. When you wake the next morning your mind is
buzzing with new, still more ingenious and extravagant
scripts.

An active organism does not simply dissipate its energies; emotions channel the currents. Euphoria and torment, sensuality and rapture thrust it into the thick of
the world. An emotion isolates an object or event and
brings it into focus: it dramatizes. It pulls away what Vir-
ginia Woolf called the cotton in our days, the stretches of
time when, doing what there is to be done, our eyes are
cloudy and our hearts muffled. The emotion frames,
crops, views that object or event from a distance or in extreme close-ups, views it from an odd angle or through a
slightly open doorway, as reflected on the surface of a
pond or in a mirror, in the mist or in the shadings of twi-
light. The emotional energies charge that object or event
and make it shine and glower, purr and howl. The active
force of emotions makes us act in the romance, comedy,
tragedy, cosmic or mercantile epic, melodrama, or sitcom
they improvise as they go.

Only those subjugated to the dour discipline of common sense conceive of laughter and tears reactively—
laughter as a relieved, tears as a panicky reaction to a
failure, a local breakdown in the network of reason and
order. Hilarity is active, the sentient organism jaywalk-
ing across the teleological grooves, teasing out mulishness

and asininity in the diligent machinery of the industrious city. A cockatoo awakens before dawn, spreads his glamorous plumage, hurls himself into somersaults around his perch, engages another in mock combat, and sets out to see how many new vocalizations he can come up with in a half-hour screaming jag. An hour later, he will alight to pick a few seeds out of the dish and take a sip of water. Despite the Aristotelian theory of catharsis and the Freudian theory of cathexis, emotions are not dissipated in being released, but escalated. Two friends laugh when they meet, were already laughing in anticipation of their meeting, and they keep up and intensify this ebullient vitality by turning the boss's and the doctor's orders into gags, making business emergencies and domestic crises return as farces, perversely pronouncing maxims of prudence, the most sensible formulas of everyday talk, as jokes.

We stop laughing before a zany spring landscape full of scurrying ants, wallowing caterpillars, fluttering birds, the squandermania of dancing flowers scattering billions of seeds to the winds, and we set out to know. It's what we call getting serious, this will to know everything, everything about the species of animate life, two hundred ninety thousand of which are species of beetles, everything about outer space, everything about God. The seriousness in the will to know everything is the will to become everything. We spend a lifetime trying to know everything about one species of beetle, and end up with more questions than when we started; our systems encompass everything under a set of ultimate cosmic laws or an ultimate generative cause, and those laws or that cause plunge us into ultimate bewilderment. The recognition of bewilderment takes the weak form of chicken-hearted sullenness and the strong form of hilarity. The

seriousness of the will to know ends in laughter before
the spectacle of the race between the will to know everything so as to become everything and the Joker that is
death.

Blessing is the forces poured upon the fragments, rid-
dles, and dreadful accidents by a laughter that knows its
power to zigzag on and that sees things scintillate and
flare and career with its energies. A father is a blessing
for his son, not in the providential care that has set aside
savings for education, life insurance, and a trust fund,
but in the hearty laughter that sends off the youth on
his crotch-rocket bike to roar the Western highways all
summer, a laughter that will invigorate the son's own
when he laughs at all the thunderstorms, tight-assed
waitresses, and nights in jail in the months to come. A
thinker who comprehends with the hands, hands made
for blessing, sees swallows and owls, wetlands and tundra
pullulate with grace. Blessing is the beginning and the
end of all ecological awareness.

After the impotence of infancy, tears are not reactions
to breakdowns in our well-laid plans, to blunders that
leave hurts. They are not reactions to pains that we fear:
no longer caged in a cradle, our minds have learned how
to bypass the city's daily allotment of contaminated
foods, toxins polluting the air and water, and car crashes.
In the strong, active sensibility, pain ignites a black light
that steadies the gaze and the hand extended in compassion to all that suffers. Grief and weeping are active ways
we open to the pain and death of others, and if we can
grieve and weep over ourselves, it is by opening to the
grief and weeping of others over our ways. Grief and anguish open, above and below our well-policed apartment,
the sublime heights and monstrous depths where we see
the faces of people starving in the Sahel and drowned in

cyclones in Bangladesh, hear the hummingbird fallen
from the poisoned skies, water with our tears the violet
in the parched asphalt. It is bravery and strength that
weep.

Gabriel García Márquez tells of an isolated tiny village by the sea, so exposed to the winds that the gardens
are of stones and the dead have to be thrown off cliffs.
There, one day, the sea washes up the corpse of a
drowned man. The villagers gather about it and first
anxiously check their numbers to ensure themselves it is
not one of them. When they begin piously to wash the
corpse of all the tangled seaweed and clear it of the in-
crustations of ocean mollusks, they are astonished to
find it the corpse of one huge and powerful in frame,
noble in bearing, with a face so splendidly handsome
they cannot turn their eyes from it even to sleep. None
of the clothing of the villagers fits it; the women set out
to make new, splendid clothing for the dead man. The
next day the men return to report the corpse is not that
of someone from any of the other villages along the
nearby coast, and the villagers feel gratitude that it is
their corpse. The men smelt what metal they can find in
their houses to forge a weight that will take the corpse
down to the abyss below the fishes that might tear away
at it when they return it to the sea. The women walk
upland to where flowers grow. Under the bier the men
have built, they pile a meadow of intricately woven
wreaths. They give him a name: Esteban. It pains them
to return him an orphan to the sea, and they select from
the best of themselves a mother and father for him, and
others become his brothers, sisters, aunts, and cousins.
"While they fought for the privilege of carrying him on
their shoulders along the steep escarpment by the cliffs,
men and women became aware for the first time of the

desolation of their streets, the dryness of their patios, the narrowness of their dreams as they faced the splendor and beauty of their drowned man. . . . [When they had lowered him into the sea,] they did not need to look at one another to realize that they were no longer all present, that they never would be. But they also knew that everything would be different from then on, that their houses would have wider doors, higher ceilings, and stronger floors so that Esteban's memory could go everywhere without bumping into beams and so that no one in the future would dare whisper the big boob finally died, too bad, the handsome fool has finally died, because they were going to paint their house fronts gay colors to make Esteban's memory eternal and they were going to break their backs digging for springs among the stones and planting flowers on the cliffs so that in future years at dawn the passengers on great liners would awaken, suffocated by the smell of gardens on the high seas, and the captain would have to come down from the bridge in his dress uniform, with his astrolabe, his pole star, and his row of war medals and, pointing to the promontory of roses on the horizon, he would say in fourteen languages, look there, where the wind is so peaceful now that it's gone to sleep beneath the beds, over there, where the sun's so bright that the sunflowers don't know which way to turn, yes, over there, that's Esteban's village."[1]

There is no grief that is strong that does not act by casting curses. Curses are not impotent reactions to the mindless blows of adversity; they are the forces of grief that know their power to pursue the malevolent into its lairs. Face to face, you see the force of your curses shatter the composure of the one you curse. Life knows that, like tempestuous stars that produce effects across millions of light-years of empty space, its outbursts produce their effects across distance and time. Our curses drive the juggernauts of determinism that crush the innocent back into the no-man's-land of the unnegotiable and the unacceptable. Our curses besiege the oppressor, the rich one with his ill-gotten wealth—and all wealth is ill-gotten wealth in our world where forty thousand children die each day in the fetid slums of Third World cities, an Auschwitz every three months. The forces of grief that curse the human and cosmic villainy are the source of all the religion and ethics there have been and are in the world.

I came to that realization one day in Kenya, listening to an anthropologist who revealed to me how much of Kikuyu culture, ritual, and lore is devoted to detecting, decoding, and counteracting the curses that the Kikuyu find put on them in all the untoward events of their lives. How strange and unintelligible to us, I said, this belief in curses; in our Western modern life we call the police to neutralize our aggressors and take steps to be able simply to avoid people who might wish us evil. Our religion has monotheized, she answered, all the evil eyes and baleful voices that their culture finds among the powers of all living things. Our science, she pointed out, explains all the breakdowns in our dysfunctional sexual, psychosomatic, and professional lives by citing the power of malignant words cast on us, words that pursue us long after those who have cursed us are dead: the *No* of the father and the *I do not love you* of the mother.

There is no laughter without tears. The events we only laugh at are spectacles and the companions we only laugh with are playing roles. The man who never cries never laughs and can only chuckle, guffaw, and snicker. Grief preserves the laughter of the child or the hero who died, and will hear that laughter again. Grief over the

murdered Tupac Katari or Che Guevara breaks into
laughter as his martyred blood seals pacts in the High
Andes and ignites fire-bombs in the base camps of the
CIA. There is no cursing without blessing, and every
blessing is a fate and a curse. The rage against the
whisky-drinking, cigar-smoking evil old men in the corporate board rooms sanctifies the savage adolescents in
the slums. The Himalayan sublimities are also ice storms
and avalanches.

But to this one, exhausted and prostrate on the battlefield of so many violent and contradictory emotions,
comes at length the decision for armistice and negotia-
tions. In horror he pulls back, fists clenched, from the
sleeping woman in his bed. He inventories his resources,
counts his wounds, asks in anguish: To what end? To
what end? He calls for outside arbitration. She is not,
after all, he asks any available Kissinger, the most beautiful woman in the world? How many women are there as
intelligent, as witty, as foxy in bed? Have I not been making melodramas of her quite ordinary faults, salting the
wounds from her dime-store whips? The lures and the
hurts are set apart, put in perspective, assigned their just
proportion. Things are put in context: she is not a goddess or a demon, she is an assistant professor working on
tenure. It is what we call getting objective. Do not laugh,
do not weep, do not bless, do not curse, said Spinoza, but
understand. Understanding is the identifying, measuring, coordinating work done on the booty in the hands of
stalemated and depleted armies.

This harmonizing knowledge does not give rise to
serenity; it follows emotional exhaustion. It does not give
rise to evaluation; it is a systematic enterprise of devalua-
tion. It does not result from reflection; it is driven by the
recoil of resentment and rancor.

Worn out by so much folly and flailing, you take stock
of yourself. You set out to identify your needs and wants;
you identify yourself as a set of needs and wants. Dis-
pleasures demarcate the lacks and the emptinesses. You
set out to identify the initiatives and acquire the skills
needed to obtain what you need and want. Contentment
is the feeling of closure and sufficiency that simmers
over some content assimilated. Displeasure and contentment are reactive feelings, forces that weaken.

The content assimilated neutralizes the agitation of a
want, and the sodden contentment draws life inward and
uses life's forces to maintain this saturation. Resentful of
disturbances and resentful of the time that washes it
away, contentment engenders images of enduring content and integral satisfaction, images of happiness. These
images are its ideas and its ideals, against which the
events that form and dissolve on the river of time—passing from being into nothingness—count for nothing.
The agreeableness with which pleasure conforms itself
to what is given is a force of mendacity. The eyes sodden
with contentment see the laughter, tears, and curses of
the others already fading into nothingness. Contentment
makes itself vulnerable.

The weak sensibility cramps in reaction to frustra-
tions and aggressions. The sensitive substance, recoiling
from the impact of the outside force, finds itself in misery, backed up to itself, mired in itself. It deals with the
impression left by the aggressive blow struck from outside, the aftereffect or image of that blow, and not with
the aggressor, who has passed on.

In a social gathering, you find yourself exposed to a
caustic or demeaning remark cast your way. Had you
been strong in social skills, you would have met the blow
with a repartee that would have ended in laughter. Had

you been very strong, you would have surprised the aggressor with a put-down so witty he would have found himself unable not to laugh at himself. But you could only mumble something witless, and the fencer turned away to a worthier opponent. You feel wounded, mortified. The blow was delivered, and the aggressor turned away; the feeling does not pass. You find yourself unable to be fully present to the sallies and rebounds of the crackling banter about you. Back in your room, unable to sleep, you go over the wound, probing it, feeling it, verifying the pain. In the trace of the aggression you secrete the image of the aggressor. Having been unable to parry the blow at the time or answer it with a counter-blow, you strike out at that image: you disparage, denigrate, vituperate the other, not in his presence but in his image. It goes on for hours, for days. How much longer and how much stronger resentment is than was the pain felt in the encounter itself! Your impotence to engage the aggressive force and discharge the pain prolongs itself in this stoked violence. Resentment secretes images that obscure your view of the present and distort your memory of the past. Resentment is a positive force of mendacity. This vindictive force weakens your active forces; you will be the less present at the next social gathering, the less self-assured, the more vulnerable to the next one who probes into your reserve, whose wit—to which you do not riposte—becomes aggressive. You will be identified as thin-skinned and moody; in reaction you will identify yourself as civilized and sensitive. You will barricade yourself in that preposterous condition known as self-respect.

In our pains, become rancorous, in our pleasures, become requirements, we make our bodies vulnerable, we formulate our identities as needy and dependent and servile. We demand to be protected and to be gratified. We subjugate ourselves to the exacting discipline of common sense; we make ourselves useful. We offer ourselves to being used.

The garrulousness of contentment and resentment have covered nature with their text. All the other animals and the plants, the savannahs and the deserts, the oceans and the skies have been labeled, measured, inventoried along the coordinates drawn by the cravings and exactions of contentment and resentment. The contented mind views everywhere its own grids. The resentful heart finds the world a complex of threats, shelters, and compensations.

Laughter and tears, blessing and cursing break through the packaging and labeling of things that make our environment something only scanned and skimmed over. They are the forces with which we impact on nature, which we had perused only as the text of the world. They are forces that seek out and engage reality.

At the cocktail party or singles bar, you are on the lookout for the woman who materializes your girlfriend or wife fantasy. You set out to lure and settle her into your own bed, apartment, and domesticated retreat from the world, where she will be the medium for your self-recognition in daily conversation where everything she says responds to what you say, think, and fantasize. But you do not know a woman until you find yourself blessing the universe and her because she has made you laugh and laugh at yourself, until she has made you cry, until you find yourself cursing her and yourself because she makes you weep as no hammer-blow hurled at your thumb or collapse of all your investments ever has or could.

Blessings and Curses

How reckless and violent is the compulsion to open our eyes and face what happens, what is! Philosophers have described truth-seeking as a breaking into, a taking apart of things, a violation of the taboos with which ancient reverence had surrounded them. But to seek contact with reality is to expose ourselves not only to the hard-edged resistance of things but to being pained and exhausted by them. We would not know what happens if we did not know extreme pleasure, if we did not know extreme pain! It is because we sense that the only way to know what we are capable of, what we care about, what we fear, is to plunge into insecurity, loneliness, hunger, and cold, that we leave home to hitchhike across the country. We go live in such wretched places—Haiti, Bolivia, Salvador in Brazil, Congo, Bangladesh—places whose culture is in ruins, whose people are destitute, diseased, and despairing—because just staying in the safe and comfortable places, at home or in the developed countries, is to skim over reality.

There is an inner momentum in the appetite for reality. When you go off to live in the mountains, you will long to hike all the trails, sleep in the rainy spring nights and winter snow, and climb all the cliffs. Once you get a feeling for the sea, you long to sail and dive the oceans. Lust is not content with respectful and considerate caresses and release of tension; it wants another, wilder orgasm, it wants orgasms on jet airplanes and in tropical swamps, it wants bondage and whips. You get sick of the glut of cities, cultures, nature converted into edited and framed and narrated images in the cathode ray tube; you want to climb Machu Picchu, get lost in the favelas of Rio and the slums of Calcutta, get dysentery in Kabul and crabs in the bordellos of Marrakesh, sleep weeks in the Amazonian rain forest, and ski Antarctica.

The strong emotions seek out what is incoherent, in-
consistent, contradictory, countersensical; they endorse
what is unpredictable, unworkable, insurmountable, un-
fathomable.

High-spiritedness seeks out the nonsecured, the
bungling, the dumb luck, and the nonsensical in nature.
It relishes the absurdity of any system in which everything works. In every hilarity over a priggery or a fritz-
out there is an Ionescoan hankering for absurdity that
takes on cosmic and metaphysical dimensions.

She sees you have nothing else in your hands and are
holding open your wallet; she does her smile and says,
"Is that everything?" not because she thinks you are
holding some more minimart items behind your back,
but because the marketing experts have programmed her
mind to suggest that there may be other things in the
store you might buy. You look outside at your motorcycle
engine running in the exploding summer: all this schem-
ing, all this calculation and programming, how the sun
out there is laughing! A colleen whose smile is flashed
and voice programmed by the computers of capitalism,
ridiculous as a fox harnessed into a dogsled—you love it!
"You're right," you say, "I forgot the *National Enquirer*
and the *Wall Street Journal*!"

The hands that are made for blessing extend ever
wider, spread a rainbow over the foolish eyes of a cater-
pillar and the fumes of the departing motorcycle, and
find again the gesture of the Aztec priest on the summit
of the blood-soaked pyramid spreading wide his hands to
the four corners of a universe where all is fragment, rid-
dle, and dreadful accident.

Weeping can come to an end, engulfed in exhaustion,
in a new grief, or in a new joy. But every grief, even the
smallest, is inconsolable: not even the fledgling sparrow
we find dead after the storm is replaceable. Every grief

reaches out to a universe ruled by arbitrary gods or a universe where tragic gods are chained to desolate cliffs and torn apart by vultures.

Our curses over localized malices, when an outbreak of emotion expels them, invoke the gaping black hole of everlasting torment. There is a vertigo in the cursing voice, sending its echoes to the infernal abysses.

We lose ourselves in our emotions. Euphoria does not glow inside, a contentment simmering over a content secured within the closed doors of our body. You exclaim: How good I feel this morning! but when you turn back to your feeling, trying to observe it, you find that this euphoria without object fades away. The euphoria streams through you from the rondos the sun and wind are playing in the meadow. You no longer have a sense of yourself as a discontinuous entity agitated with needs and tasks.

The euphoria escalates by isolating a figure outside ourselves—a trout leaping in the cascade, a toucan in the forest canopy, a cobra bracelet about the ankle flashing under the folds of an Indian woman's sari. The whole is fragmented; the fragments drift and collide as enigmatic strokes of luck and calamity. This figure outside us becomes an incendiary point and an open floodgate through which all the tumultuous energies of our euphoria pour.

Every emotion is a letting go of the supports and the implements, a giving way of the ground under our feet, a vertigo. We say we "fall in love"; love is not only something that befalls us, from the outside, something impossible to produce by planning; it is also itself a fall. It is through erotic passion that the other is other—goddess and tigress, god and wolf. If physical love is the most intense pleasure we can know, it is because we are never more vulnerable than when we fall in love. In the suffocating ardor of eroticism, we understand the injunction to ruin ourselves in order to love. To love—that is, to pour kisses and caresses, tenderness and torment upon someone we have come upon by chance, making that being lose his or her head in a sacred and demonic wasteland where that being will be lost to us.

Our torments and exultations exhaust themselves; our laughter and our tears die away, our blessing and our cursing are carried away into the enigmas of the future and the silences of the past. Blessing the small birds that fly in the winter winds, cursing the wrath of the terrible deities, does not aim to ensure our salvation, and it does not do so. The one who laughs or who curses before the firing squad does not defeat death nor devise a resurrection. The laughter and the curses in the faces of the torturers are ways of discharging one's forces, of dying.

Everyone who acts well learns detachment from the results of action. Every doctor who acts well, every scientist, musician, thinker, lover, and parent comes to understand how attachment to success ruins every action. One's name is written into the successful action, and insidiously gleams forth, tempting the statesman and doctor into actions that are manipulations and the musician, scientist, and thinker into entertainment, propaganda, and ideology, the lover and parent into possession.

Before one's failures as before one's successes, sound instinct impels the doctor, scientist, musician, or thinker to withdraw from action and abandon oneself to the rain of falling leaves in autumn forests, on mountaintops sprawled naked under the sun, in the depths of tropical oceans where one's hands light up the ephemeral flares of phosphorescent plankton. The abandon to the mineral and briny pleasure settles into the flesh, disconnects the thoughts, the plans, the inner chatter of the mind, and issues in the sense of the dissolution of oneself. Sound instinct leads one further: to the abandon of all internal probings and speculations about one's own nature, the abandon of all efforts to map out one's inner darkness, the refusal of all temptations to turn the light into that darkness.

6

Violations

What proves to me that the figures I see in the street outside my window are not hats and coats covering robots
driven by springs is the fact that, taking the sounds they
make to be intended as words, I find a coherent meaning
in them. I verify my impression by asking the speaker if
this is what he meant. For me, whatever utters a coherent set of words, and further sets of words coherent with
that set, is someone with a mind like my own.

But isn't a knowledge of other minds required before
language can function at all? The words are only sounds
in the air unless we take them as uttered meaningfully
by someone, just as marks on paper cease to be stains, and
marks on rocks cease to be the effects of erosion when we
take them to have been intended by someone to designate something to someone else.

> Words deny and lie. Language is so essentially a
> power of contradiction that, instead of saying that
> language is the way we recognize mental beings,
> should we not rather say that language is the way
> what others have in their minds can always be fal-
> sified?

We recognize as another human someone with whom
we can speak; those whose tongue we do not or cannot
learn are babblers and barbarians. But conversation with
someone whose tongue we understand comes to an end
when that person makes truth claims based on his or her
tribal ruler, ancestor, or deity.

Violations

Something new dawned in the history of the human species, Edmund Husserl wrote, when men in Athens, conversing with foreigners, began giving reasons for the ways of Athenians. Until then, to the questions of foreigners—Why do you think as you do, do as you do?—the answers had been: Because our fathers, who founded our clan, nation, city, have taught us to do thus. Because our gods have said this. The men called philosophers set out to give answers that those who did not share those ancestors, who did not have the totem gods of the Athenians, could accept, reasons that just anyone, anywhere, with insight could accept. The practice of giving, and demanding, reasons, reasons that anyone with insight would endorse, breaks through the particularities of languages, traditions, and customs that not only shape the way in which what we know is formulated but that shape our very perception of things. This new discourse gives reasons for each of its assertions and submits each of its reasons to judgment. It admits anyone endowed with insight as its judge. It invokes, Husserl said, the idea of humanity—universal humanity, rational humanity.

But as scientific discourse extends ever further the range of things for which it supplies reasons, the reasons supporting assertions about microscopic and macroscopic entities become ever more complex, and a proportionally ever smaller part of it is accessible in the discourse of any scientist or man in the street. We call ourselves rational when we can justify a small part of our discourse with reasons, but those reasons are reasons only because they can be justified by verified observations, laws, and theories which we assume others could supply. Our rationality functions to castigate as backwardness, mythic, and fanciful the discourse of others we sense to be at variance with that small part of our discourse we can justify with reasons—reasons whose justification we take largely on faith. Our rationality invokes the notion of universal humanity only to exclude many of our interlocutors from it.

How eccentric of Hegel to have imagined that when we go to encounter others, it is recognition we demand, recognition of the freedom and self-consciousness of the ego, confirmation, attestation, certification of our identity!

Is it not instead the others who demand that we identify ourselves? "Last week you said you would. . . ." "But you are now a mother. . . ." "But you just said that. . . ." "How is your dissertation coming along?" "You said you loved me. . . ." Our interlocutors seek coherence, a line of intelligibility in the phases and states of our duration. They seek to link up our past with the present, to know the future as what we say now commits us to.

When we respond to these demands, our words are so many positions, postures, we take before this witness. "Yes, last week I said I would, but here is what happened that made me realize we should not do that." "Yes, I am now a mother, but that does not mean I am giving up my course work at the university." "I said that, but what I meant was. . . ."

How burdensome, how tedious, how vacuous it is to have to maintain all this identity, all this coherence, all this deployment of reciprocal recognition! In fact we get facetious. "Did I say I would last week? I forgot." "Yeah, now I'm Doctor Sweeney. But doctors in English literature don't make house calls, and most of our patients are dead." "Sure I said I loved you; otherwise you would not have written my term-paper for me."

Violations

Morality takes thought and action to be polarized by the notions of good and evil. It assumes that we act in order to maintain, secure, or acquire what we take to be a good. Goods, as the goals and results of actions, are durable goods; they must at least endure the time it takes us to reach or take possession of them. And they should contribute to the conservation and preservation of those who acquire them.

Morality enjoins us to subordinate our forces to that good; the one who acts makes his or her organs and faculties serve to acquire something. The action narrows down and focuses our forces.

The violation of the existence and natures of things, of oneself, or of others is evil. Disrespect encroaches upon the space of others, and alters or empties their nature. Respect is respect for the limits, the boundaries, the space of others, and thus for their natures. Morally good action designates the active respect for others, for things, and also for ourselves.

Sometimes people seem to have found the formula early in life and they apply it with equanimity until they die: they are genial, affable, helpful. Others find the method is good sense: before any problem, their own or that of another, they appraise the issue, survey the alternatives, select the best one, and do not worry over it if, as often happens, the best available decision does not work. Does not the majority of people with whom we converse fall into these categories—the kind ones and the sensible ones? Trivializing, leveling kindness. Shallow, self-justifying sensibleness.

Respect for the other, for the sincerity, honesty, and integrity of the other, is said to be essential in the practice of discourse. There is no conversation, it is alleged, unless we, first, take what the other says to express the integral application of her sensory and mental powers to what she has seen and experienced, and, second, try to see what is true in what she says. Without abandoning our liberal concern for the plight of unwed mothers and sick immigrants, we must try to see the valid point the conservative is making.

It would seem that respect which initiates conversation is real only at the far end of conversation, when we have come not only to understand the informative content of what our interlocutor has said but have also come to understand the speaker's background, priorities, and competence.

Extending this model of conversation, as moral and altruistic, one constructs a moral formula for sexual intercourse. Violence and pain must be excluded. A force hurled at us becomes violence when it violates our inner space, when it violates our integrity and what we call our person. We respect the physical integrity of another by respecting her or his person, and we do that by respecting what she or he says. Sexual intercourse must be conducted by lucid conversation, where the integrity of each is affirmed.

> What is awkward in this morality is that we ourselves, in conversation, do not want to be treated in this moral way. We went to Tibet to be uplifted and were deeply troubled. After returning, our head is still spinning, and we meet some stranger who, we hope, was there longer and saw more deeply than we did. We tell him, I went to the Potala, to the gompas, and I walked through room after room crammed with huge gold- and jewel-encrusted statues almost all alike, down corridor after corridor frescoed with intricate paintings of religious scenes that duplicated one another endlessly; I saw stupas covered with two tons of gold; I

saw thousands of scroll paintings. This is supposed to be Buddhism, which teaches that everything we can see and touch is illusory, teaches that desire for such things is suffering and that blessedness comes through a complete liberation from attachment not only to all things we can see and touch but to this world and this life itself! I felt like John Huss in the palaces of the Vatican. If our interlocutor takes it to be paramount to show respect for our honesty and sincerity, takes what we say to contain a truth, then the conversation is nothing to us. What we are on the lookout for is someone who can contest not only what we say but what we saw and felt and experienced. Who can show us a totally different way to look at the wealth, the superfluous, unproductive art treasures of the monasteries, and the life of those professed Buddhists. Who can show us the stupidity in our thinking, who can send us back to really look. If we do not find such a one in person, we search for him in the books about Tibet.

It happens that we come upon someone who does not simply expose to us our obtuseness and stupidity and send us back to the monastery to look again, but exposes also his own mortifications, humiliations, and wounds. Who shows us that after a year, after ten years in a monastery, the art treasures of the monastery leave him devastated, emptied. The divestment, deprivation, and abnegation of the monks, now that he has tried to join them, to measure his strengths and determination to theirs, have left him abashed, mystified. When we meet such a person, perhaps the conversation does not serve us, is not useful for communicating more intensely with Tibet and its monasteries. But the conversation, in which each does not recognize himself in what he is saying, is a summit, a vortex, and a black hole of intensity.

And what else is erotic craving but a craving to be violated? In voluptuous turmoil, we are left not simply wounded, but shattered. The violent emotions that are aroused, that sense the obscenity in anguish, that push on in a momentum that can no longer derail or control itself, sense also the exultation of risking oneself, of plunging into the danger zone, of expending our forces at a loss.

Is it not in nonsense and indecency—in laughter and in erotic excitement—that we, rather than recognize, re-cognize, one another, find ourselves transparent to one another? And is it not this transparency that precedes the assumption in language that I am addressing someone with a mind like my own?

We see whoever laughs as one like us—even if we do not see what he or she is laughing at, do not see what is funny. And we are drawn to anyone who laughs by a primary movement of sensibility. Human interattraction is not at bottom a fearful and cautious alliance for purposes of mutual defense and cooperation in work.

You have for hand baggage a double paper shopping bag with an old sweat shirt stuffed on top. You are in the airport in Sendai, in the worn and crumpled clothing Americans often wear for long trips, even in other countries. It is the day after sarin gas was released in the Tokyo subway. You notice some Japanese turning furtive, wary glances at you. There are no seats; you push to the back of the room and sit against the back wall, trying to be invisible. A Buddhist priest comes into the hall, his simple white and black robes and sandals emanating confident assurance, impeccably clean. His serene demeanor seems fixed on timeless things. He does not see your leg

stretched out on the floor, trips, catches hold of a bystander, but as he does so two bottles of Chivas Regal fall
from his robes and smash on the floor soaking you in an
alcoholic splash. The crash, but even more the spreading
smell, strange for a waiting hall in an airport, freeze the
bystanders in a panic. Then laughter breaks out, spreading
wider as people get up to see what is going on. Laughter
rises and falls and rises again as eyes meet eyes. The priest
himself and you are laughing when your eyes meet.

In each individual, the laughter is now no longer
pleasure over the unexpected, the incongruous, but pleasure over the dissolution of boundaries, of clothing, of
the body armor of strangers in an airport, pleasure over
the evident pleasure of others. It makes the object or
event that unleashed laughter slip from attention and
sets into motion an intense communication.

If the priest had tripped and smashed his smuggled
Chivas Regals in the toilet, he would not have laughed.
Awkwardness is transformed into clowning, distress into
exuberance, in the transparency of each to the others.
And the gratuitous release of energy in laughter gives
even the priest a sense of adolescent insouciance beyond
what the bottles of Chivas Regal had promised. The
laughter is felt by all who are caught up in it as a surplus
of energy that was in them despite the fatigue of the
night, despite the new security constraints that will af-
fect their lives and yours. How we feel and see all this
surplus energy when, ten minutes later, the flight is an-
nounced and everybody grabs their bags and jumps up
with adolescent gusto!

Erotic excitement arises by contact and spreads by
contagion, making us transparent to one another. A bare-
breasted woman is dancing voluptuously in the street
in Salvador during Carnaval; we fix our fevered eyes on
her and feel a current of complicity with the men and
women about us, white or black, adolescent or aged. We

find ourselves aroused by feeling the warm thigh of the
dozing passenger next to us on the bus, as we are not
aroused by the warm vinyl of the bus seat. During rush
hour when we are standing in a packed subway car, we
feel a ripple of excitement when someone's fingers
lightly brush the inside of our thigh. Whether we are
male or female, we feel aroused when, leaning over a
gable, we see in the neighboring yard a woman
sprawled on a towel spread over the summer grass, plea-
suring herself. Though we are straight, we feel our
penis pulsing when we look over some rocks on the
summer beach and see the lifeguard naked and
writhing under a gleaming erection. In his *White Book*,
Jean Cocteau drew a picture of an aroused penis and labeled it: The part of a man that never lies. Whatever
the educated, disciplined, decent mind may say, the
penis stiffening, the labia and clitoris throbbing with
blood and excitement and pleasure affirm, "Yes I like
that, yes he or she is my kind, yes I am attracted to him
and her."

Language, where all the words are common words, is
not a means for the ego to be recognized as a pole of
unity and also uniqueness, is not a means for my peculiar
identity to be confirmed, attested, and certified. It is in
tears, and in passionate rejection, that I experience my
separation from others. But tears and passionate rejection
do not bring forth some positive traits that make me appear to myself to be distinctive and distinct.

When my home burns, when I lose my job, when I
discover that the investment scheme in which I put all
my savings is a swindle, my desolation, finding expression in tears, contains the sense of the extreme difficulty
of replacing these things. How immediately others understand those tears and, with them, all the significance
that my perhaps ordinary house had for me! When, at
the limit of frustration over finding myself unable to get

anyone else—my family, my friends, my therapist—to
see my point of view, to feel the gloom of my depression
or the edge of my exasperation, even though I am using
common words which everybody understands, I break
down in tears, these tears affirm not the unique traits by
which I am positively distinct from all others, but how
incomprehensible it is to me that what I feel is incomprehensible to others.

Is it in passion, rather than discourse, that we demand
to be separated, distinct, and distinctive? In love we find
ourselves the object of an extreme and exclusive attachment on the part of another. We bask in finding our
principles, our values, our troubles taken seriously by at
least one person. In denuding ourselves before one another, we take off the uniforms, the categories, the endurance, the reasons, and the functions with which our
existence had been clothed. I denude myself before my
lover, as she or he before me, and expose to the other all
the singularity of my frame, my pitted, birthmarked,
and scarred skin, as so many signs of my singularity and
irreplaceability.

Passion pursues the denuding inward. Our sense of
ourselves, our self-respect shaped in fulfilling a function
in the mechanical and social environment, our dignity
maintained in multiple confrontations, collaborations,
and demands, dissolves; the ego loses its focus as center of
evaluations, decisions, and initiatives. If I draw out of our
mutual exposedness something to hold on to when we
part—if, for example, I take from it a sense of my reality
and my worth—this reality and worth become laughable.
How ridiculous is the man who would say: Well, she gave
me proof that I am the most important man in the world!

We realize that what was at stake is unidentifiable,
ungraspable, when the intimacy of our communication
is broken—by death, separation, or a misunderstanding.
The break is identified not conceptually but in sobbing:

inarticulate cries of anguish hold on to the moment when the communication broke and what it awaited never arrived. In sobbing I realize that what I have lost by this death, separation, or misunderstanding is not something we had. In desolation I feel forever gone something that our weeks, months, years together had not yet made real, something that foresight, planning, and projects did not outline and make clear—what passion divined only as an abyss of chance and luck.

In fact, does not the temptation to see in someone's attachment to me evidence of my exceptional reality and worth spring from the fact that I had not been able to justify them to myself by positive traits I had seen in myself? And do I not find myself consolidating and promoting my separate existence at the expense of others? The very sense of having a separate existence can be malevolent and pernicious.

The sense of having a separate existence, throbbing in tears and erotic rejection, cannot take being an improbable and irreplaceable I to be a good. Still less, to be the fundamental good that I seek in discourse and in passion. I am attached to my separate existence, improbable and irreplaceable, but would I be if I were not certain that I could just as well laugh at it? In laughing tenderly over my awkward and bungling adolescent horniness, in guffawing over my melodramatic love affairs, I become attached to them and to myself.

We laugh at "Freudian slips," when someone utters something he had no intention of saying; we are sure that what came out is what he really thinks or feels. We laugh at a kitten falling over itself in playing with a ball; we feel that we have just gotten a glimpse into the real nature of a young animal, of the young animal. We laugh at people whose oafish or slobby bodies are ridiculous, whose lives one cannot take seriously, whose jobs or careers are a joke, and who died in some glitch of the

Violations

machinery, of nature, or of their own program for surviving. However miserable I am when my lover has left me
for someone else, feeling that there was something
uniquely in me that deserved so extreme and exclusive an
attachment was, I plaintively realize, laughable. On our
honeymoon on the island of St. John in the Caribbean
there was that sign on a rustic hangout: You're here with
only the hurricanes and the hangovers, two thousand
miles from self-importance. What else can we do, do we
do, but laugh, when we face the improbability of our
birth, the ludicrously squalid death we are heading for,
the filthy corpse our vaunted and incomparable existence
is going to turn into? This laughter at the I, at the demand the I makes, laughter over one's birth, over one's
death, need not be ironic or bitter. It can be as light as the
laughter with which we greet the fanciful anatomy of a
preying mantis or dragon pipefish, the pompous assertive-
ness of a bumblebee, the birth of a baby crocodile.

Looking at oneself while laughing turns into an
erotic vertigo. How we are lustfully drawn to our own
mouth that, in the mirror, we see wide open, exposing
the wet, lascivious tongue! We stand in front of the mirror looking at our legs shaking, our belly rolling in peals
of laughter, and, unable to stop ourselves, we stroke that
belly, run our hands up between our thighs, fall back
upon the bed. They fix mirrors on the ceilings and on the
walls around the bed in bordellos so that we will be able
to see the awkward, unmanageable contortions and flail-
ings of our body and not be able to avoid laughing, and it
is this, and not the simple sight of our genitals, that will
jiggle us into the abandon and anonymity of orgasm.

And is it not by not taking ourselves seriously that we
enter into conversation? It is with horseplay or farcical
comment about his looks or about our own activity that
he has interrupted that we greet a friend or the plumber

or our father-in-law. When we meet Jamaican reggae musicians, Brazilian capoeira fighters, Haitian practitioners of Voodoo, or specialists in some sector of our white mythology of reason, the first thing we do is use language to unleash a laugh.

We use words to get to laughter, and laughter generates words—words that set forth and share—consecrate—the things that left us abashed, disconcerted, disheveled, the events that did not enlighten but delighted us. Linguistics misses this use of words when it envisions words as discriminators, functioning to delimit and contrast. Language, like everything real, is based on positive entities, the positive, positing words that illuminate and consecrate. Words do not simply isolate entities by contrast and delimitation; the radiance of passing strangers, birds, trees, cars, and landscapes resonate in their tones and accent. Their inner pacing and resonance pick up that of the languidly sprawling summer landscape, the secretive and melancholy Medieval town, the vast desert under sheltering evening skies.

There is never a perfect fit of words on the things they designate; they are GI uniforms pulled over the gawky bodies of adolescent recruits. And the words are never completely artless; their meanings seethe with allusions and equivocations, their inner pacing and resonance connect with one another in haphazard short-circuitings. And so they are prone to bring out the awkwardness and bungling in the things they designate— the pretenses and the prankishness of things.

How transparent we are in laughter, and how understandable are our tears! We share one another's sorrow. Mourning is not a way our psyche, unable to confront the loss of a lover or the death of a friend, closes in upon itself to conserve that lost one in our memories. Most of us first mourned in childhood for a squirrel or a bird which we came upon dead on a wooded path, a creature of which we had no memory. The grief and weeping open upon the void left by that loss or that death. How visible is that void to the compassionate eyes of others!

As we advance in life and adulthood, we weep over the loss of lovers and the death of friends. We also grieve over gifted young people we never met who are struck down in accidents or in crippling diseases; we grieve over young and old heroes in remote lands who arise from nowhere and are struck down in noble and lost causes. Indeed it is in our grief over these heroes that we feel the loss and death of those we have known.

As laughter generates words, words that consecrate, words of blessing, weeping generates words, words of imprecation, words that curse the human and cosmic villainy.

It is not in a discourse that demands and gives reasons for what we saw and did, and reasons for those reasons, that we recognize our common humanity. If we open a conversation with someone, it is because first we see him or her as someone with whom we could laugh and grieve. Prior to the speech that informs and the speech that directs and orders, there is the speech that articulates for those who were not there, and articulates further for those who were, what we laugh and weep over, what we bless and curse. Our speech is polarized by the grand things, the blessed events that come as surprises and accidents from the outside, and by the sinister things.

Laughter and tears, blessing and cursing, give birth to the primary operative words of language—the value terms. *Great, beautiful, strong, healthy, delicious, wild*—all of our conversations weave about such words. The value terms are not labels that record observations or gauge gradations and comparisons. They find their meaning not in comparative sentences but in exclamations: How healthy

I am! How strong I am! How happy I am! How beautiful
I am! How good it is to be alive! We say these things because we feel them, and by saying them we feel still better. There are people who have no positive notion of
health, for whom health is only the absence of illness,
who regard themselves as healthy only after the annual
checkup when the doctor has reported that no foreign
bodies have been detected proliferating and all the vital
functions test within the statistically average range.
There are people for whom health has a dense and radiant meaning, for whom it is the sovereign value—men
sprinting up the steps from the gym after a workout to
muscle exhaustion, women setting out on their vacation
to trek the Andes, adolescent boys on Patagonian ranches
breaking the young bulls for rodeo. The value terms are
not forms that inform and classify; they are forces: the
beautiful words make radiant the one to whom they are
said and make gracious the one who says them, the noble
words ennoble, the healthy words vitalize, the strong
words invigorate; the ugly words befoul, the servile words
demean those who speak them, the weak words enervate
and enfeeble, the sick words contaminate. The value
terms concentrate our superabundant energies within us;
we channel those energies outward in our hands made for
blessing and in the cursings that come from our heart.
Saying "How happy I am!" we leave our happiness on
passersby hailed, on the trees and the clouds, in flowers
left on the formica desks of offices.

Is it not because we recognize someone as one with
whom we could laugh and grieve, speaking of absurd
and of heartrending things, that we believe the reasons
we find or construct will be recognizable by all those
with whom we speak?

To enter into contact with someone is not to conceptually grasp his or her identity and respect his or her

boundaries and inner space. We greet someone with
"Hey man!" The vibrant tone of those words hail in that
individual a man, not a child, a student, or a waiter. We
address and answer someone in the words and forms of
speech that are his or hers. We catch up the tone of the
one who addresses us, his or her voice resounds in our
own. We catch the urgent, frantic, panicky, exultant, or
astonished tone. To answer the frenetic tone of a young
person with the stentorian tone of officious and sedentary life is, before we refuse to really understand what we
are being told, to refuse his tone; it is to refuse him.

The tone of the one who addresses me does not respect
but pervades my inner space. His sounds are in me now,
my body has become his. Inhaling and exhaling the air,
the drift of pheromone, catching hormonal rhythms, my
breath and his commingle in the atmosphere about us.

When we attend to someone who greets us, it is not
to require confirmation, attestation, certification of our
identity. To respond to someone who greets us is to drop
our concerns and thoughts, and expose ourselves to her.
It is to expose ourselves to questioning and judgment.
Simply responding to her greeting is to recognize her
rights over us. Each time we enter into conversation we
expose ourselves to being altered or emptied out, emptied of our convictions, our expectations, our memories.

When we get together we talk about individuals we
have seen or heard, or heard tell of, who exhibit extravagant health, sumptuous beauty, smoldering eroticism,
bravado. These are also the people we talk to when we
get together. In speaking with the father about his fool-
hardy and impudent son, we call forth the brash youth
in him; in speaking with our suburban neighbors of
the vixen we saw performing in the night club on our
women's night out, we call forth the glamorous and seductive women in them.

Violations

Truth begins in conversations, shared laughter, friendship, and eroticism. But other people are not just other
perspectives, other points of view, bearers of other data.
How reckless and violent is the will to open one's eyes
and face what happens, what is, among them! It is this
reckless and violent will we seek contact with in them.
We would not know what happens among them, if, exposing ourselves to what happens, what is, we did not know
extreme pleasure, if we did not know extreme pain!

That is why so often the most moving, the most unfor-
gettable conversations we have are with strangers, people
from another land, another age, whom we have never seen
before and will never see again. We seek communication
with those most unlike ourselves; our most important conversations are with prostitutes, criminals, gravediggers.
We seek to be freed from the carapace of ourselves.

Only a streetkid dared to go talk with Edson Cordeiro
after his concert in Sâo Paulo; only an old peasant woman
dared to speak with subcommandante Marcos. For us
to speak with them, we would have to be impetuous as
youth, insolent and shameless as the old woman who has
decided that at her age she can do what she likes.

To communicate effectively with those who fascinate
us is to break through their integrity, their natures, their
independence, their autonomy—to wound them. Communication through these breaches in our psychophysical
integrity turns in a vortex, heedless of the consequences.
Communication is not itself a "good." It excludes any
concern for the time to come. It excludes any concern for
our interests. Thus we are drawn to all who face what
happens, what is, and who suffer.

7

Innocence

You were born in a Reno hospital, you were born in a dusty shack in a nameless favela on the outskirts of Rio de Janeiro. How extremely improbable is your existence! There had been the chance encounter of that woman with that man—out of the two and a half billion men on the planet, the happenstance that she pleased him and he her and that they disrobed and copulated, and then the fluke that of two hundred million spermatozoa repeatedly ejaculated into her vagina this *one* met with and got absorbed into this ovum. With the slightest alteration at any turn of the path, made up of a million chance encounters, it would have been someone else, not you, who was born.

The number of atomic particles in the universe is said to be ten to the seventy-sixth power. But the number of possible combinations of the human DNA molecule is ten to the 2,400,000,000th power. The odds of being you are one in ten to the 2,400,000,000th power. Before it happened, it was exceedingly unlikely that what was born would be you.

For you to look back to the time before your birth is to look upon an abyss in which you are utterly absent, nowhere programmed, nowhere preexisting in potency. Beneath you, behind you, there is nothing that forecast you, demanded you, required you. Behind you, you feel this void. You were born and appear in the world as a will-o'-the-wisp hovering above its interconnections and gearings. Before the solid determinisms of the world about you, you cannot shake loose a sense of inner insubstantiality. You feel yourself drifting and bouncing over

Innocence

the interconnections and gearings of the world. You are a precarious power without a past, come out of the void, existing in defiance of this void. There is something ineradicably heroic about your bare existence. You are seduced by this heroism, born by chance from the void. That is why something understands, something quickens in you, whenever you hear of a heroic act.

What a stupendous marvel, your birth in a Reno hospital, in a dusty hut in a nameless favela! What a marvel, the newborn, the born new! And what innocence! How light is your birth, not laden with the weight of a past it has to answer for! In the past with all its crimes, all its outrages and villainy, there was nothing whatever of you.

You open your eyes. Everything is new! The immense white light floods you; where there was nothing at all there is suddenly this vision, these endless landscapes, these fathomless skies!

We sometimes say that the newborn has awakened to the world, that, at the moment of conception, life awakened in the chemical jelly of the egg. It is not as though life was there, but sleeping, before. The expression rather reflects our deep sense that awakening is a being born. The luminous consciousness that in the morning awakens to the bedroom flooded with light is as innocent and new as a baby robin that has just broken the shell of an egg.

Everything is present without past or future. Upon awakening, the unconsciousness of sleep is disconnected; the empty space in which it existed is utterly lost and our eyes cannot see where it has gone. The cold, the dark, and the damp of the night have passed away without leaving a trace. We open our eyes and at once find ourselves immersed in light, the phosphorescent surfaces of things and glowing horizons extending about us. We awaken in warmth, air, resonance, grounded on a dimension of support that extends indefinitely before our steps.

Innocence

The elements are there, incessantly oncoming. The light of yesterday and of a minute ago are utterly passed away; there is no residue of them in this light. The light is so fully there it conceals the horizons of its own future. It is there without reserving anything for tomorrow, without guarantees, there by gratuity and grace.

Once awake, we move on, noting the familiar patterns and general lines of the house, the landscape, and the workplace. Immersed in continuities and recurrences, the state of awareness persists listless and drowsy, as though drunken. But in the course of a day there are dozens, hundreds of soberings up, awakenings. It is one thing to take note of things, of landmarks, our glance passing lightly over them as we move among them. It is something else to wake up to them. While reading on the porch, to wake up to a hummingbird sizzling in the sheets of sunlight. To wake up to the grain of the old wood of the porch railing, enigmatic as a fossil of some long-extinct reptile.

The momentum of what has come to pass does not launch the force of awakening; awakening is a leap out of that momentum. The flow of nonapparition in the night—or the continuum of appearances in the day— are interrupted. A cut, a break is made, and across this gap the past passes out of reach. The force to make this cut is what Friedrich Nietzsche spoke of as the power of active forgetting—the power to wipe away what we have just passed through. The awakening comes as though from nowhere. We shake our head and peer about to find where we are.

Awakening is a bound, not weighted down with the past that inculpates the present and demands compensation from the future, a bound out of the drunkenness of remorse and resentment. Awakening is a commencement. It is a point of departure. We come alive; we become alive to the dragonfly, to the twisted grain of the porch railing. Awakening is a birth.

Awakening is joyous. The innocence of awakening, the active disconnection from the past, make possible this joy. How good to be alive! How refreshing is this silence! How calm the morning is! How pungent it smells! In every joy there is an awakening.

Joy is truthful. Joy is affirmative and self-affirmative; we cannot not believe our joy. We cannot not believe the visions joy illuminates. For joy opens wide our eyes to the surfaces warmed and illuminated but also to the shadows; joy gives us the strength to open our eyes to all that is there without being foreseeable or understood.

Awakening is proud and hopeful. The interruption of continuity makes possible the leap, with all the forces of the present, into what is ahead. It makes possible hope, the awaiting what cannot reasonably be expected.

The interruption of continuity, the effacement of the past—innocence—also makes pride possible. Men would like to think that they became functionally male with the mounting saps of their biological maturation; it gives them the confidence that they are males by nature. Women would like to think that their female nature is the natural accumulation of biological developments. But in truth the story of a boy becoming a man is a tale of one awkwardness, failure, castration after another! How a woman forgets the ignorance she groped in as a girl! None of us could know one moment of sexual happiness, one moment of pride in our animal sexuality and nature, if we remembered, if we did not have the power to forget. What will always bog down the orgasmic ecstasy is the memory that compares you with the woman last night or last month or the fifteen-year-old of my first summer of love. What fades the presence of the lover in our arms is the performance that makes our

Innocence

kisses and caresses a demonstration of something that
had been in doubt, our pleasure a compensation for the
stresses and distresses of the day and of the years. The
force to forget that melancholy succession of mortifications that is the history of each of us is the great power
that makes us able to make love tonight as though we
had never made love to anyone before, to make love
tonight as though there will never be anyone again; it is
the ecstasy that says I was born to be here, in your arms,
I could die now.

Yes, awakening can stop and silence us, freezing the
continuity and momentum of movements. To wake up to
birds in the forest or in the sky we immobilize all our operations, become trees or mounds on the grassy knoll. In
this paraplegic state, excitations flicker across our sensibility with the flitting of warblers through the foliage,
eddies of exhilaration in us turn with the soaring of
frigate birds over the waves and through the storm
clouds. To visit the coral fish we abandon our upright
posture and all our grasping and manipulative faculties
and drift with the surge.

Awakening can also give rise to action. What we call
our action, in the intense sense, is not simply an adjust-
ment to compensate for what passes and passes away—an
inhalation that compensates for an exhalation, a stabilizing step forward that compensates for the destabilizing of
our gait, a day that brings a day's work to be done equivalent to the day's work that was done. Our action rises
from an interruption, a break in the continuity of biological, physiological, and also workaday operations that go
on in us.

Philosophies of history, whether reactionary or radi-
cal, see in the end achieved by action a value, a good,
which is a predicate constructed in the categorical system
of an industry, a society, and a culture. They see in the

Innocence

directive force of an action a meaning that operates only within the vocabulary, grammar, and rhetoric of a semiotic system. They see in the driving force of an action the momentum of accumulated skills and habits. They explain an action out of an evolving environment where everything is already social, significant and historical.

But our action is an interruption of the continuous dialectic of history, an awakening from the drowsy murmur of the semiotics of a culture. Its bound of energy comes from a break in the continuity of skills and habits. Each moment of awakening is a return to youth, to the insolence, impetuousness, brashness of youth. In our action there is festivity, license, and puerile pleasure. There is an element of lubricity, of wickedness in the innocence of action.

Our action breaks with the past, with the morose succession of mortifications, subjugations, enslavements, those of childhood and those of colonialism and capitalist exploitation, from which we rise up to stand as a man and as a woman. Our action breaks with the present and its future, to give the forces of our care and our protection to an ancient tree, a species of animal life endangered by industry and urbanization, an ancient sensibility surviving in an old Guatemalan town.

My action arises when I wake up to *what I have to do*. In the action the I awakens.

What I want wakes me up to what I have to do. I have to collect wood and clean and skin the fish if I am to cook them. I have to buy lumber if I am to build this house. I have to work out these mathematical data if I am to know how much lumber I will have to buy. In working out this mathematics, I have to follow the rules for calculation.

But what I have to do may conflict with what my desires and even my needs induce me to do; it may postpone or interfere with what I want to do and with the urgency of my hunger and thirst. What has to be done imposes itself; it is, in Immanuel Kant's terminology, not hypothetically but categorically imperative. I wake up to the intrinsic importance of the reality in front of me, which is in danger, or to the intrinsic importance of what needs me in order to exist. Urgency imposes what has to be done. Immediacy imposes it on me.

Are there not innumerable such cases among our actions? Ancient burial vaults that surface when I begin to plow this field dictate what has to be done now. Strolling in the sequoia forest, I come upon a discarded, still smoldering, cigarette butt in the dry leaves. I am here, and what has to be done has to be done right away. But also *I* must do it—because I can. Running as I do each day in the forest, I have the strength, which the old couple who stopped me do not have, to free the deer caught in the branches of a tree in the flooding river. Someone in cramps or panicking is in danger of drowning, and I am the one who can swim. This hitchhiker in Morocco is not clad for the night cold now descending, and mine is the only car on the road.

A dancer heads for the studio for the day's work, ignoring all the tasks and pleasures she could share with others, distractions that solicit her on the way. In the studio *what I have to do today* is clear to her and undeniable. It is also clear that she has to be a dancer—not because she aims to get rich and famous, but because dance must exist and her body is made for dancing. Paul Gauguin abandoned his family in order to pursue his art. "I am moving next month to Fatu-iva, a still almost cannibalistic island in the Marquesas. There, I feel, completely uncivilized surroundings and total solitude will revive in me, before I die, a last spark of enthusiasm which will rekindle my imagination and bring my talent to its conclusion."

Innocence

Everyone who is engaged in a work that is important knows the clear sense of *what I have to do*—a fireman in a city and a guard in a lookout in the Himalayan forest during the dry season, a retired person living by the sea where the sea birds are engulfed in an oil spill, an Aymara in Peru caring for the patch of land and pair of llamas given him by his father.

Anyone who spends a weekend camping in the sequoia forest will never again leave it. She will care for the sequoias till the end of her days and feel indignation whenever she hears of some puny human who claims them as his private property and plans to cut down these twenty-five-hundred-year-old trees for his own enrichment.

What I have to do is determined not only by what results can come from my skills and resources. I have to stay with a dying friend, though the doctors and nurses have done everything that can be done. I have to stand for a minute of silence during the burial of children killed by a gunman in another country. I have to grieve for the plundered forest.

When I decide to do what I want, I discover what I have to do; the layout of implements and obstacles before me commands my action. What we want is not determined by a fiat of our free will. How often is what we want determined by training, habit, lack of imagination, or obscure and unconscious fears! How often, when we feel we can do whatever we want, we find that in the course of doing it the enjoyment has faded away! How much of what we do we do only to make the time pass! To make the time pass until a friend comes, until we get sleepy enough to go to bed, to get through the summer, to fill up retirement. Is it not that I discover what I want to do only when I discover what I have to do?

Innocence

What radiance when we see someone doing what he really wants to do! In conducting the diving expedition with all the knowledge and skill that piloting of the boat and managing the scuba equipment require, in protecting those on the expedition against mishaps and showing them how to see the marvels of the ocean, the divemaster finds that being a divemaster is what he really wants to do. A woman finds in her heart a song that is hers alone to sing, that the world has never heard, a song that will never be heard if she does not sing it. A man finds in the surface and depth of his body the excesses of a passion to love, to squander kisses and caresses upon strangers, upon animals and hills and the fog, a passion that has never before been felt in the heat of the whirling universe, and he knows that if he does not pour forth this passion and this love no organism ever will. In leaving overpaid private nursing of the pampered rich to care for the wounded and the famished in a refugee camp, a nurse finds that she is doing what she really wants to do.

The awakening to *what I have to do* is an awakening of emotional forces that drive our action. They rise up and break through the webs of meanings spun by ideologies, preconceptions, and justifications. All the most ancient emotions awaken, are newborn, as though there had never been history. Before the death of our child, mourners gather in a tragic chorus, as though there had never been the Christian doctrine of individual immortality or the secular doctrines of the biological insignificance of any individual of the species. In the heart of the rain forest, we feel the ancient emotions felt by hunters and gatherers a million years ago around campfires and in rituals and dances. By night the computer programmer and office manager dream the sacred and demonic emotions of ancient myths. In our posts in industrialized, rationalized, corporate society, we feel the fierce passions of outlaws and bandits.

Emotions awakened by the importance, urgency, and immediacy of what has to be done give our actions their youth and innocence. Despite Socrates' slogan *An unexamined life is not worth living,* despite Kierkegaard's replacing love with the unending examination of love's intentions and motives, we do not admire and we do not trust actions that issue from intentions rationally justified and as the conclusions of reasonings from principles. We entrust ourselves to divemasters in whom clairvoyant attentiveness and courage are instinctual. Nothing is more flagrant than courage, which we do not see in front of us but feel pulling at our heart. So transparent is courage that when we see it in another we feel the pounding of that very courage in us. We give our trust not from dependency on another's courage, but in a surge of courage in ourselves. It is not virtue we admire, but natures, people with sound instincts. We do not entrust our children to the care of a mother who pursues an interminable psychoanalysis of her conscious and unconscious motives—and we wish we could spare her own. We trust the woman with the big heart—the farm woman beaming over calves, piglets, chicks; the aging prostitute longing for nothing more than to give tenderness and love; the woman in the old folk's home watching the children play in the park across the street and caring for her old cat. Our trust is an upsurge of instinctual love in us which understands her love.

How strange is the notion that the extraordinary is not required! Why do we say that heroic or very fine actions go beyond what is obligatory or demanded? Why do we say that from an ethical point of view such actions would be agreeable or worthwhile or a good idea, but

that they are not required? Why are people greatly admired for actions they would not be blamed for omitting?

We may refrain from blame because we recognize the
uselessness, indeed the harm, of inflicting guilt on someone who failed to do the extraordinary thing, or because
we fear we too might fail to act. Yet the death in hideously
painful disease that may well await us will require no less
heroism than is shown by the guerrilla in battle or before
the firing squad; attending to our dying lover or child may
require of us the unimaginable strengths and resolve of
those who go on rescue operations in glaciers or medical
missions in refugee camps. And when the time comes,
though others be silent and without reproach about us, we
will know that the heroic is obligatory.'

If we fail to rise to such an occasion, the reproach will
be waiting on our lips one day—the day of our dying if
not before—even if we have spent our whole life ensur-
ing that no extraordinary demand is ever put on us, that
we could answer every situation with ordinary decency.
To live our lives doing what work we do only the comfortable and secure way, to put forth only to a measured
and prudent extent the powers and energies and feelings
we have, is to suffuse our years with an inner desolation
that will become irremediable when old age irreversibly
diminishes those powers and energies and feelings. To
have lived our life without ever having stood for something exceptional, something noble, consigns us irreme-
diably to a wretched evaluation of our life.

Actions leave you empty when you do them. You happened to be there at the right time, somehow said the
right thing to the youth, were able to pass him on the
money for the tuition in such a way that he would take
it. It needed to be done with a lot of tact and secrecy to
be done right, and any lifting of that veil of secrecy
would spoil it now. Prostitutes understand that, covering

Innocence

their kind hearts with harsh and cynical words. You are left the next day emptied, your good deed more a burden than a glory, the glory of it surely a burden, not left with strengthened powers but with harnessed powers, not knowing if new powers, the right powers, will be there when the time comes.

We live our lives on the surface of the planet, among things we can detach and manipulate; we live under the sky. The sky is without surface, without shape, without inner structure, ungraspable. We see in the sky the sovereign realm of chance. The sky is also a bond uniting us to all who breathe under its expanse, uniting us to all who are born and shall be born under that sky.

Chance confounds the intellect, the reasoning, reckoning intellect that identifies possibilities on the basis of past regularities. Chance excites us, quickens the will. In pursuing actions that expose us to the blows of chance we know in exhilaration what we have received by chance, what we are by chance. The will drawn to chance is what we call love.

Love is awakened only by chance. In the fugitive, suffocating beauty of a woman's body, astonishment greets the utterly improbable. Nothing is more contrary to love than interrogation, than trembling before the unknowable, than wishing unfavorable chances be excluded.

Also in the empty sky above us, we see a realm of terror, terrorist death that strikes at random, strikes without consideration of innocence or guilt, strikes anyone who just happens to be there.

Courage courses in the resolve of one faced with the imminence of death, who seizes hold of all that is possible by mobilizing all available resources. When there are no adequate resources, no forces you can count on, when you stand under the empty and terrorist sky, what surges up in you is bravado.

Innocence

In many cases it is necessary to hope for nothing in order to undertake any action. It is by finding the weakest link in the oppressive system that revolution becomes possible, but to him who sees the technology for and the will to control annealing every link in our chains, only revolt is possible. In the dungeons of the tyranny, the prisoners form networks and commit themselves to physical exercise. As the villagers flee the plague for which there is no cure, the old woman cooks food to bring to the victims.

Bravado defies, provokes, and challenges death. There is something infantile about bravado. Bravado turns the eyes upward into a sky as empty of you as was the surface and depth of the earth before you were born. Bravado swells in feeling seduced by your heroic existence born by chance in the void.

8

Catastrophic
Time

How strange that the sequoias of California, which live
two thousand five hundred years, die! Lightning has
struck each of them innumerable times, burning the
dead wood of their cores, without killing them. For nothing, until humans invented chain saws, can kill a sequoia.
When they die, they die of a natural death. Their seeds
were from the start programmed for them to live twenty-
five hundred years and then die.

There is a specific duration, a lifetime, intrinsic to all
living things. Whenever we see plants or animals we see
infancy, youth, maturity, aging, and dying.

The perception that evolved in living things is not
only a seeing and touching of other things. There is no
perception without a perception of time. Plants have no
recourse but to undergo whatever befalls them, rain and
sunshine or scorching sun and tornados, but animals,
which can move, are able to flee. They feel fear, they
sense they are vulnerable, they sense the imminence of
their death. Those that care for their progeny, as well as
those that do not, have a sense of their own infancy and
of the infancy of their offspring. They see, in their own
species and in other species, infancy, youth, maturity,
aging, and dying.

This biological time intrinsic to their natures can be
transformed into a field of work in some organisms.
Work circumscribes and structures time.

A human primate detaches something—a loose
stone, a branch, a pipe wrench—from the continuity
of the natural or fabricated environment. With his tool

he detaches himself and shifts his view from the environment continuous with his body to goals or results beyond it. Between his tool and the goals or results he sees a relationship of means and end, cause and effect. The identification of distinct substances, and the understanding of a relationship between means and ends and between causes and effects, is the core of reason. Everyone who works is rational.

Knowledge is not given to us in a sudden illumination of the mind; to know is to strive, to work. We learn that this chipped stone can serve to cut and to chop; that stone, blunted, can serve to grind. We learn that this is iron and that is sulphur, by putting them successively in reactions with other substances. Once we see what we can do with a broken branch, a chipped stone, a bone or steel knife, we figure out what falling rocks, streaming water, the roots of trees do by themselves.

We work in order to maintain, secure, or acquire what we take to be a good. Goods contribute to the refurbishment and protection of those who acquire them. Something acquires value by being promised in the future, and by withstanding, and helping us withstand, the passing of time, by enduring.

The human primate makes of himself a tool; he inserts himself into the field of work and reason as an implement that can be used to reach ends, a cause that produces effects. The order of means and foreseen results, of causes and effects, enters into him. His mind turns into a place where his limbs and senses are subordinated to purposes, where his present consciousness is subordinated to an anticipated future. What has come to pass in his body—his strength, his skills—and in his mind—his memories—is subordinated to the future. His enterprise, all his efforts, require the future to make sense.

The one who works maintains a sense of individual identity, by envisioning himself in the future. I identify what I am doing by specifying what I shall be doing. It is tomorrow that gives sense to whatever I do today; it is tomorrow that gives sense to whatever I am today.

The one who works envisages others as collaborators or as obstructors. Our workspace, however much it is our own, inevitably finds itself surrounded by the workspaces of others whom we have to count on, at least as unwitting accomplices. Like tools, they stand detached and destined for results and products, for a future. The results and products they are working for, their futures, give them individual identities.

In the shifty eyes of others, in their duplicitous movements, we sense a disaster that could befall us through their negligence, or a malevolence or madness that could single us out. We detach ourselves from them, and also detach weapons we could use against them. Words are among these weapons; each of us has in childhood learned the words that can hurt others, more deeply than sticks and stones. But with our work we build walls too to contain their violence.

Work extends, circumscribes, and delimits a zone of time. The future is articulated as a field of possibilities, the past as a field of resources retained in our know-how and skills.

Work is measurable as a half-day's job, a day's work. The movement of the sun across the sky or a pointer round a dial can be marked in hours, minutes, seconds, nanoseconds. Equivalences are virtually interchangeable: a day, as a day, is interchangeable with another day, an hour with another hour. This equivalence and interchangeability of measurable segments of time make the events that take place in those segments appear from the

first as repeatable, reversible, and repairable. To survey
the time of the world is to see to what extent the succession of things can be reproduced, varied, and reversed.

Death strikes. Death suddenly strikes down a collaborator. Death does not annihilate her; the body is there and
takes up as much space as before. But death violently and
at one blow destroys this worker's future and strips of
their meaning, not only the undertaking she was engaged in when it struck, but retroactively all the work
that led to it. Death strikes in the now, and immediately
drives its shock wave into the future and down the past of
that life. Death strikes, reducing to nothing the instru-
ment she had made of herself in the world of work, reducing to nothing her individual identity. She died from
an infection picked up while working in the emergency
room. He fell from the scaffolding of his half-built
house. Her half-completed medical education, his half-
finished house, appear as intensive efforts that, had this
outcome been foreseen, would never have been made.

When someone we know dies, we weep: it is impossible that she should be dead. We say over and over again, I
can't believe it.

It is unthinkable that this companion, this associate,
is dead; to think of him, of what he was, is to think of
him as a being whom we identified from the function
which the field of tasks before him and the future ahead
of him gave him. Whenever we think of him now, we inevitably think of his image, his ghost, his soul still in-
volved in his concerns. If we think of our dead parent or
lover, we think of her watching us or speaking to us as
she used to do. We think how proud our father would
have been to see us at this law school graduation; we see
again in a spasm of perfidy and shame our dead lover as
we sell his motorcycle to pay for computer programming

lessons. But this sense of the ongoing existence of the dead is accompanied by the knowledge that death has annihilated the possibilities and tasks of their future. The ghost or soul we visualize when we think of the dead one is a trembling, vacillating vision that darkens the world of work and reason.

A catastrophic event destroys the time of work and reason, and opens upon the empty endurance of void. Duration, beneath or without any things that endure and that pass and without any processes, is not, as Immanuel Kant thought, given from the start in a separate intuition. It is caught sight of in an event—a catastrophic event which strikes down a companion, annihilating all his future and nullifying all his past.

The death that strikes this associate of ours and the death that strikes someone elsewhere are events separated by stretches of duration. The later death is not the effect or the result of the earlier one. The deaths that come to pass do not accumulate like resources. The expanse of duration between them is empty of them.

The death of a collaborator gives us an unnerving premonition that a like violence—a heavy or sharp tool that slips, an automobile collision, a microbe—could abruptly befall us in our time and space of work and reason, and could annihilate, along with our future, the significance of our past. A violent blow can also destroy our future and past without destroying the present, as when an automobile accident or disease paralyzes the hand of a music student or a surgical intern.

Violence may erupt in a fellow worker, who strikes out amok and abruptly destroys our future. A war breaks out, and we find ourselves drafted into the front lines, or a foreign power begins shelling and bombing the towns and homes about us. A revolution breaks out and, in the fever of revolt, we throw our investments, our homes, our

122

Catastrophic Time

families, our lives into the chaos and violence of the insurrection.

We cannot imagine our dead companion and imagine him annihilated, but we cannot imagine our own death without imagining ourselves cast into the empty endurance of the void. Yet in dying we are not liberated into the abyss of empty time; we sink into the dead weight of a corpse. Fatigue and aging, which make us feel encumbered, held back in the spring of our initiatives, by the weight of our bodies, make us feel already the corpse that death will turn us into. An infected wound makes us see, smell, and feel the decomposition and corruption already at work in our bodies. We die like dogs, befouling the ground and poisoning the air.

It is not only our own death that destroys all the structure of intelligible time in our lives. Our life can be so intertwined with that of our child, everything we do motivated by the future of that child, that when she is killed in a hit-and-run accident, not only her future, but our own and our past, are devastated. Our life can be so spliced onto that of our lover that when a stray bullet in a street leaves him paralyzed and in an iron lung, not only our plans for a future together, but our strength to pursue any plans, are obliterated. Sometimes it is some nameless and unidentifiable anxiety that cuts an untraversable abyss between us and any promises or lures that extend a future, and makes of our life an empty desolation.

The time that orders the future, present, and past in which we work appears to us to be linear. It also appears to us to exist on the surface of things and on the surface of Earth. It appears superficial when a catastrophe reveals the time of the empty endurance of the void. This empty endurance appears to us to be deep, the void an abyss. It lurks in the depths of Earth.

Work detaches things from the surface of Earth—
plants, animals, branches, and loose stones used as tools.
We detach ourselves by standing back, supported by the
expanse of the surface of Earth. The first fires to be used
appeared on the surface of Earth, but they came from
the storm clouds, and seemed to bring to concentration
the inner heat of the ground. At length workers began to
disembowel the earth to pull forth ores to be smelted
with fire into iron and bronze. Fire and iron made more
effective tools; they especially made devastating weapons.
Previously, people had turned their tools as weapons on
one another; now a torch thrown burns down a whole
hamlet and its field crops; a raid with metal weapons dis-
embowels everybody who fights as well as all who flee.
In raids, pillages, and massacres with fire and iron, catastrophe erupts in settlements.

We work on Earth's crust; we see movements of
Earth's substance—shifting continental plates, earthquakes, volcanic eruptions—that are calamitous for us
and for innumerable other living organisms. In the lightning that sinks into it and in earthquakes, geysers, and
volcanic eruptions, we sense all the inner incandescence
of our planet. We sense that only on the surface is Earth
a crust that can be turned into enduring goods, that beneath the deepest mines there is the inner core of fire.
We sense that Earth is a particle of the sun, separated
from the sun in a cosmic explosion. We see that it is in
the midst of a cosmic cataclysmic time that our work extends its transitory and vulnerable intelligible time.

The corpse is there, it has to be washed, the casket has
to be selected and paid for, a hall has to be reserved and
a meal arranged for those who will come to the funeral.
A preacher will be hired to tell of some real or imagined
achievements, which some of the family and friends

recall from the life that was snuffed out before it got anywhere, and deck them with the names of exemplary
virtues. Willy-nilly, we bridge the calamity, as though it
were but a temporary setback in the open road of intelligible time.

Back from the funeral, we think we felt the grim
reaper swing close; we feel him stalking us. We ward off
anxiety before the imminent and inescapable annihilation awaiting us by establishing control over our life and
field of operations, by projecting an advance representation of what each day brings, and by measuring our enterprises to our forces. We arrange our home and our situation and our workday in such a way that we retain,
behind the forms of our performances, a reserve of force
for the tasks that will recur the next day. We settle into
an occupation that requires only those mental tasks for
which we have already contracted the mental skills. We
frame our pleasures and our angers, our affections and
our vexations, in the patterns and confines of feelings we
can repeat indefinitely. We avoid going to places utterly
unlike any other, which would leave us wholly astonished, with an astonishment that could never recur. We
seek out partners others might also fall in love with, and
we love our partner as others love like partners, with a
love that we could recycle for another partner should we
lose this one. For we sense that were we to expend all our
forces on an adventure, discharge all our mental powers
on a problem, empty out all the love in our heart on a
woman or a man unlike any other, we would be dying in
that adventure, that problem, that love.

Alternatively, sensing the imminence and inevitability of the disaster that will annihilate all our forces, we
resolve to activate all of them in the present. We commit
all our forces formed and shaped by past events and give
their skill, sensitivity, and momentum to our present

work. We make the work before us the condensation of all the works we ever wanted or shall ever want to accomplish. A jazz musician sets aside all the concerns of others to improvise his own song now, with the sense that he does not have time for business investments, does not have time to get a job teaching the music of others to others, that he has to make his music now. He improvises with all the resonance of his birth in a certain family, a certain ethnic group, a certain neighborhood, and puts into his composition all the yearnings, hopes, and heartbreaks that have shaped his sensibility. A gymnast goes to the bars and rings each day with the sense that she was born with this exceptional body, in this place on the planet where the gym and the trainer are available, and does not have time to take a full liberal arts course, does not have time this afternoon to go to the picnic with her housemates, because the gymnast in her will be dead by the age of twenty-one. The guerrilla sees all that is possible for his country in this revolutionary moment, and all that is possible for himself, and takes all that he has lived through and suffered and learned from childhood as preparation for his decisive and dangerous mission.

The citizen-activist, statesman, or guerrilla fits the day or years before him or her into the broad time of history. The possibilities for which she marshals her resources may not be possibilities that will become actual for her; they may belong to her comrades, to the next generation, after the victory has been won, a victory for which she may well have given her life.

The sense of the imminence of disaster transforms the intelligible time of work, and of history, and gives us the sense of the time of our own life. I see the trajectory of time from my birth to my death and I situate on it all the initiatives I now undertake. My sense of coming to an end, of ending, is what gives my life the sense of ends,

of goals, and makes me determine initiatives that are determinate. I act resolutely to bring the momentum of all
that has come to pass in me into my acts, and I extend
my acts unto their ends. For me living becomes the living
out now of all my powers, discharging all my forces in
my present work. Living is dying on my own and with
my own forces.

Witnessing a fatal accident on the highway when coming
back from the office, we pull our minds back to where
we have to go tonight and back to driving the car. We
awaken after the heart attack and find ourselves paralyzed on one side and half blind; as the shock levels out,
we begin to think of how we will manage. Awakening on
a stretcher after a battle, come to the realization that we
will most likely not leave the field hospital alive, we
think of disposing of our savings for the use of those
who will survive us. We lay out works that will consume
our life, and count on there being others for whom maintaining the fertility of this farm, managing this business,
reading books will be significant. Ecologists today speak
urgently of the steps that will have to be taken lest pollu-
tion, destruction of the ozone shield, and the greenhouse
effect put an end to human life, even all life, on this
planet. Astrophysicists who speak of the inevitable extinction of our sun hold open the possibility that before
that happens we may well be able to colonize other plan-
etary systems around other stars. They count on thought,
scientific-technological thought, which arose and arises
out of work and operates in the service of work.

   Though the sense of imminent—and inevitable—
disaster may drive us totally and resolutely into the intelligible time of work, the time of work cannot be shielded
from the fall of a heavy or sharp tool, an automobile col-

lision, a microbe, or the violence that seizes a collaborator or a passerby, those occurrences that drop us into the time of the empty endurance of void. Yet the catastrophic time that devastates us can also strangely hold us, and even draw us into it. There are drives in us that let us be drawn into catastrophe, that live in catastrophic events.

We had long planned this trip to New Orleans, California, Paris, or India. There, our education would flower, we would find the exciting people, we would find a real life, we would find love or enlightenment. But once there, we found the streets, the buildings, the roads, the landscapes alien and indifferent to us. No opportunities opened up before us. We did not connect with people, find friends or a lover. We saw that the streets, buildings, and landscapes looked bleak and harsh to those who lived there. The men and women looked preoccupied and weary; their routine lives without urgency or glamour seemed empty and sad. We who had left our job and our place in a mediocre community found our life diminished just by observing the barrenness of people's lives in these narrow confines, the pedestrian neighborhoods and landscapes that had been so mythologized. We found ourselves in a state of detachment and anxiety, disconnected from any initiative or adventure, and feeling the emptiness of our days.

One rainy evening, we were seated in a bus. We were not on a trip heading for some opportunity—only returning to our rented room again for the night. We looked out the bus window into the rain and the fog. And then our eyes got absorbed in the trees emerging from the fog, their branches almost bare of leaves now with the oncoming of the winter. The splay of their branches was different for each tree, not foreseeable, and as they emerged into view they were already passing out of view forever.

Memory retained no hold on them. Along with the patterns of the trees emerging and passing back into the fog
without meaning or function, we felt the empty endurance of the void. The bare branches emerging and
fading away filled all our consciousness, so that we no
longer felt a separation between them and ourselves. We
felt desolate, barren, alone, but the strangeness of these
barely substantial trees in the fog brought a sense of gentle melancholy and a wistful serenity.

Along the Pacific coast of Peru is a narrow strip of
land, walled in on one side by the Andes, and exposed on
the other to the ocean, kept cold all year by the Hum-
boldt Current coming up from Antarctica. The air over
this coastal strip, heated by the sun, expands out over the
cold ocean, so that moisture from the ocean does not drift
back over the land. It never rains; most of this coastal
plain is drier than the Sahara. To the south the land is
geologically very unstable; you cross the desert utterly
devoid of vegetation, even of cactus, stretches of white
volcanic tuff poured out by some eighty-five volcanoes.
You reach the brink of Colca Canyon; it is the deepest
canyon on planet Earth. At the bottom winds a river, fed
both by melting snows from the Andes and by deep
ground water. How wrong David Hume was to declare
that causality is a mental diagram we construct and project over material reality, which is merely present and
nothing but present! In Colca Canyon we cannot see
without seeing causality. You cannot look without seeing
the successive layering of rock and lava, the cross-sections
cut in them and the scalloping of the exposed edges by
the shifting of the continental plates and by wind and
water erosion across millennia. Your slow and wearing
descent into the canyon, the grit crumbling under your
shoes, measures the time of your effort and of your life

against the geological epochs of the planet's crust and
rock layers. The scale of the Andes and of the canyon di-
minish you. The scale of geological time diminishes you
and destines any footprints you leave here, indeed any
works you build in your lifetime, to erosion and mineral
decomposition.

There are some Indian hamlets at the bottom of the
canyon. These people were passed over by the Inca empire and are too alien and too poor to be enlisted in the
Peruvian state today. You are able to find lodging for the
night. You are awakened several hours before sunrise and
led by your Indian guide up the river and then up the
canyon wall. By the time the sun has risen you have
reached the point where the canyon is deepest. Your
guide book says that the Grand Canyon of the Colorado
is 1,638 meters at its deepest; here Colca Canyon is 4,174
meters deep. It is also very narrow, a knife cut through
sixteen thousand feet of granite, at the bottom of which
like a crinkle of mercury you see the river. All around,
the glaciers of the Andes begin to blaze with the rising
sun. Loftiest is the volcano Mt. Mismi, whose melting
glacier is the source of the Amazon. Billowing in the sky
are the sulfurous fumes of the Sabancaya volcano you
passed hours ago in the dark. You are seated a very long
time on a boulder in this uninhabitable mountainscape.
No human enterprise could take hold here; you could
form no project here, not even an exploratory hike. Even
if you had any shreds of vocabulary of his language or
he of yours, you would not have anything to say to your
Indian companion, not even any question to ask him.
The discursive movements of the mind, staking out
paths, laying out positions and counterpositions, are silenced, deadened. As soon as the sun has emerged over
the peaks of the Andes, it turns the whole cloudless sky

magnesium-white. Its radiation spreads over your face and hands like warmth, although the thin air your heaving lungs are pumping in is cold. After a long time spent motionless, you are aware the sun is now high in the sky.

And then, well before seeing it, you are aware of the condor, like a silent drum-roll in the skies over the glaciers. Your eyes are pulled to a speck taking form in the empty radiance, imperceptibly becoming bigger, becoming a great bird never once flapping or even shifting its wings, soaring down from a great height and then into the canyon, descending to eye level in front of you before gradually descending deeper and becoming lost to sight. It is the first condor you have seen, with its fifteen-foot wingspan the largest flying bird on the planet; this one is brown, a young female surveying the desolate cliffs and avalanches for carrion. And then—an hour, two hours later?—there are two: again you know they are there well before they are visible. They are soaring close to one another, circling companionably in the airless heights. When they are overhead, you try to gauge their height, judging they are above you halfway again the depth of the canyon—that is, some twenty-four thousand feet. You, who could hardly climb much higher than your present thirteen thousand feet, feel your eyes, your craving, your fascination plunging to their almost immaterial realm, falling up into the region of death.

You are nothing but a vision, a longing, a euphoric outflow of life hanging onto the flight of the condors. Their flight comes from a past without memory and slides into a future without anticipation. You are cut loose, unanchored, without guy wires, drifting in the void of the sky. You know nothing but the flight of the condors, feel nothing but the thin icy air, see nothing but the summits and ice cliffs of the Andes and the granite walls of the canyon below your flight. You are alive to nothing but their bodies and their soaring, you are alive for nothing but for them.

The abrupt denuding of someone in our presence thrusts a small hiatus into the time of our everyday work. Yet the dense armor of taboos forged over human nudity in our society and in most societies bears witness to the catastrophic effect denuding has been felt to have, has been found to have, on the world of work and reason and on the sane identity of functional citizens.

When we go out in the street, or open our door to someone who knocks, we have first washed the traces of the night, the anonymity and abandon of the night, from our face and rearranged the turmoil of our hair. He dresses up in a business suit or dresses down in jeans; she puts on a pearl necklace or a neckchain of Hopi beads. We also dress today as we did yesterday and last year; she maintains the two-piece crisp look of a career woman with responsibilities; he wears a plaid shirt and sneakers even when coming to our dinner party in the city. In the uniform we see the uniformity of a series of actions, undertakings, thoughts, opinions, feelings, maintained for weeks, months, years, and predictable for the weeks, months, years ahead. We see the time of endurance, and respond to it.

In denuding herself or himself before our eyes and in our arms, she or he takes off the uniform, the categories, the endurance, and exposes the body substance in the pure chance of its shape and color. Of course in the gym-built musculature we see another kind of clothing, body-armor, uniform, a body reshaped to fit a model. But in the slight sag of the full breasts, in the smooth expanse of the belly, in the contour of the buttocks, in the bare

expanse of the inside of the upper thighs, we see flesh
without memory and without initiatives, without tasks or
commitments, flesh meaningless and idle.

In the bodies denuded, sexual excitement surges in a
meltdown of built-up structures. The posture collapses,
the manipulative diagrams of the limbs soften, legs and
thighs roll about, fingers and hands move in aimless, un-
endingly repetitive caresses, allowing themselves to be
stroked and crushed. The psychic structures with which
we screen, filter out, and channel the superabundance of
outside stimuli that flood our senses at all times are shattered and the stimuli flood us pell-mell. The structures
by which we fix an inner ego identity and censor out a
whole underworld of unconscious drives and cravings
buckle and crack; in sexual excitement the gates of the
lower dungeons are opened and feral drives and cravings
bound up and overwhelm our conscious intentions and
purposes.

Every breakup of equilibrium, Freud noted, has
something orgasmic about it. A child's cry lapses into
voluptuous abandon when it is rocked on the knees of its
father or thrown into the air. You get a hard-on during
the solemnity of Christmas high mass and during a funeral. In Leonard Cohen's novel *Beautiful Losers*, two
men are driving in the country, speeding; suddenly the
driver swerves off the road and hurtles the car through a
wall (which turns out to be painted on a billboard); on
the other side he turns to his friend and says, "Did you
come?" A year or so back, there was a hurricane roaring
up the Atlantic coast, heading for Boston. A few days
later, a student came to tell me why she had missed the
previous class. She had heard the news, and suddenly remembered her mother, the manager of a five-star hotel
in the heart of Boston, someone my student normally did

her best not to think of. She had grabbed her boyfriend and raced to Boston, where her mother, surprised to see her, let them have a room on the top floor for the night. There, naked against the glass walls of the room, they waited for the eye of the hurricane.

When we see the devastated banks and police stations in the wake of a tornado, as when we witness a revolution that overturns the entire hierarchy of a society, we feel an exultant wildness. It is not simply the justice that may arise from this leveling; it is a kinship with tempestuous and torrential nature that fires us; we come to understand that revolutionaries are not driven by utopian sentimentality.

Anguish is not without exhilaration when we suffer revolutions, lightning strikes, floods, shiftings of continental plates, earthquakes, and volcanic eruptions within ourselves. It is for this that we take off, leaving everything behind, heading alone to other continents where we know nobody and speak none of the languages. Doctors and nurses report that few people go into life-threatening operations feeling nothing but panic. They feel resignation, but they also feel a heightened intensity of the mind, a curiosity, and an undercurrent of exhilaration. We feel this kind of exhilaration and attraction even when we sense that the looming disaster will plunge us into pain and possibly extinction.

A spring morning when the ground underfoot, made of all that has died on the rock core of the planet, blooms with gentle flowers and the crawlers turn into butterflies; a high noon in the rapturous depths of tropical oceans, late afternoon on ice-covered mountaintops made of minute prisms projecting rainbows back into the blue sky—such epiphanies deliver us from our demand to be protected and gratified, from making ourselves useful in the relentless world of work. On the uninhabitable continent of Antarctica we see an enormous chunk of the ice-shelf break loose and with the sound of a cannon-shot slip into the frazzled water as a bobbling iceberg sending a tidal wave far out into the ocean.

Far from the world of work and reason, we are nothing but a euphoria in the limitless bliss of the earth, sky, and ocean. And this elation produces in us the brutal strength to face the agony of a universe not made for our contentment and indemnification. From inhuman distances, with the fearsome farsightedness of birds of prey we see that sinister spectacle of stupidities and deceits, pillage and tortures that is the history of our species. With soaring raptor eyes we see ourselves devouring plants, birds, fish, and fellow mammals, our earthbound organisms trampling exquisite microecosystems with each step. With fierce eyes, we see the lethal tides of summer and winter which exact agony from all living things. In the remote distances we see the skies emptied but for the stars burning themselves out as fast as they can.

Is there not something catastrophic in the very nature of thought? Thought is driven by an excessive compulsion, and is itself an excess over and beyond perception. Thinking is looking for what exceeds the powers of sight, what is unbearable to look at, what exceeds the possibilities of thought.

From the most ancient times, sages and scientists found in the stars and planets in their fixed positions and regular orbits the immutable order against which the transitions and processes on this planet and the future and past of our fields of work could be located and measured. But the factor of unity in the universe, which makes us speak of all the stars, radiations, and black holes as belonging to one universe, is only the oneness of the original explosion. The speed of the explosion was at first too great to allow any organization to form among the elements; there were only radiations of energy. As the force of the explosion dispersed through empty space, stars formed, and galaxies. Molar and molecular organizations appeared. Our solar system took form, and on Earth the patterns of strata, continental plates, climate, and very soon, the first living organisms. As the eons passed, more and more complex living organisms formed, with their development from spores, seeds, or eggs programmed from the start. Long before humans recorded history, they conceived of the growth and reproduction of organisms and recognized the movements of inorganic nature to be regular, governed throughout by detectable and calculable laws.

Yet sudden, uncontrollable events—collisions, explosions that abruptly destroy organizations, patterns, and systems—continually occur. There are shiftings of continental plates, earthquakes, volcanic eruptions, tidal waves, avalanches, floods, and lightning strikes that spread fire across savannah and forest. There are solar storms; there are asteroids that have struck Earth, causing massive extinctions of most species of its life, and others may strike again. Earth itself wobbles on its axis and in its orbit, resulting in ice ages and extinctions of species of life. In outer space there are collisions of heavenly bodies. There are stars that burn out.

The astrophysicists Fred Adams and Greg Laughlin have constructed the hitherto most complete scientific analysis of the fate of the universe.[1] The received astrophysical wisdom today is that there is not quite enough gravitational force exerted by all the matter in the universe to cause it to recollapse in a Big Crunch after sixty or a hundred billion years. Adams and Laughlin have projected the future of the universe to the next two hundred cosmological decades—a cosmological decade being one-followed-by-two-hundred-zeroes years. The current era, the Stelliferous Era, dominated by stars, began with the Big Bang ten billion years ago. We are currently midway through this era. It will come to an end when all the stars burn out. Our sun, four and a half billion years old, is half-way to burning itself out. It will eventually puff up into a red giant and then collapse into a white dwarf no bigger than Earth. In the process the sun will broil away Earth's oceans, leaving an uninhabitable cinder, which will perhaps spiral into the sun.

The next era the astrophysicists name the Degenerate Era. The mass of the cosmos will be locked up in the dim, dense hulks of failed, dead, exploded, and collapsed stars—white dwarfs, brown dwarfs, neutron stars, and black holes. Galaxies will begin to fall apart. As the degenerate hulks collide or sweep close to each other, some will move out beyond the fringes and go careening through intergalactic space, while others will fall toward the galactic centers, perhaps to be eaten by lurking black holes. White dwarfs will capture "dark matter" particles known as WIMPs (Weakly Interacting Massive Particles), which some theorists believe constitute ninety percent of the mass of the universe.

Toward the end of this epoch, about one hundred trillion trillion trillion years from now, the protons in the heart of every atom will begin to decay. The remaining white dwarfs and neutron stars will dissipate, converting a large fraction of the ordinary mass in the cosmos to radiation and ending the Degenerate Era. The final, Dark Era will consist in a diffuse sea of electrons, positrons, neutrinos, and radiation spread tenuously across an enormously larger region than exists today.

Catastrophic Time

The effect of extending our thought this far is an irremediable desolation. Yet something in us impels us to
hurl our thought that far. The thought that follows the
cosmic desolation is intoxicated, polluted, infected by
that desolation. The cosmic history extends before it with
no possible effect on our thought, on us, except this in-
toxication.

9

Beauty
and Lust

When in the course of our activities we perceive someone, we do not see him as an expanse of colors confined
within borders. We do not see others by their outlines.
We see the inner lines of their postures and movements.
We spot our mother from a distance coming down the
sidewalk, long before we can recognize the distinctive
hue of her complexion or the shape of her head. We recognize her by her walk. We recognize our friends by their
distinctive ways of striding along, marching, parading,
flouncing, sashaying, gamboling, or cavorting. We rarely
look to identify the precise color of our acquaintances'
complexions or their comparative sizes and bulk; we pick
up on the sprawling or the erect and agile way they sit;
we recognize the sweeping strokes of their movements or
their small, precise, and intricate gestures, the energy-
charged way they lurch forward or the languid, composed way they address the things they do; and we adjust
to their way of moving in everything we do and say
when we are with them. Even when we idly gaze at people in the crowd as so many drifting patterns in the twi-
light, our look shifts to the inner diagrams that animate
them.

Our perception of people we interact with, avoid, and
communicate with can be troubled by a sexual motif. We
sense in them a pattern that accentuates the erogenous
zones, the lips, breasts, thighs, and genitals. We follow
more loosely the practical diagrams of their posture and
gestures; our attention to the coded and expressive patterns of their facial muscles and hands slackens. Our eyes

are not really undressing the other and visualizing this
pattern. But the pattern of holds and orifices we sense in
another pulls at our lips, fingers, breasts, thighs, and genitals. We feel latent movements in our hands and genitals
troubling the axes of our posture, movements that rise to
make contact with the sexual physiognomy of the other.
When we do make contact, caresses disconnect our hands,
eyes, and postures from the tasks and attractions in the
outlying practical environment. The objects and objec-
tives of the outlying field soften, turn into drifting patterns, dissolve in a heavy and turgid atmosphere. Closed
to the outlying field of urgencies and demands, coupled
with a body corresponding to our own, the sexual embrace and penetrations find contentment in the opaque
flesh filling our orifices and engulfing our probings. Each
one feels the eddies and ripples of pleasure that intensify
the sensual contentment, a spiraling pleasure arousing
and aroused by the pleasure of the other.

There is the pleasure of doing a difficult job well, the
pleasure of keeping a tight ship, the intellectual exhilaration of solving real problems by the use of the mind.
There are pleasures that are productive and instructive.
But voluptuous pleasure is laughable pleasure. The awkward thrashings of people copulating, not keeping track
of their own limbs, liberates their laughter. Already the
gleam of eagerness and desire in the eyes provokes teasing and giggles.

Is there any pleasurable activity, any activity that
arouses laughter more than sex and eroticism? So much
the more incongruous couplings, nonfunctional couplings. Michel Foucault complained that our century,
which has invented whole sciences about sex, has invented no new sexual pleasures. Except fist fucking: a
wacky pleasure if ever there was one.

Beauty and Lust

Wasn't everyone who first tried cross-dressing or
golden showers—hey, everyone who first tried oral or
anal sex—filled with the sense that it was a gas? And an
outrage.

The serious discourse of psychotherapists, sociologists,
and ethicists rehearses the meaningfulness of the sexual
encounter. The moment of voluptuous pleasure must
contribute to self-realization. It must be subordinated to
the wholeness of a relationship, one in which the lovers
are persons. It must be subordinated to the good of society. Taking this discourse seriously, anyone who indulges
in deviant practices—masturbatory, homosexual, cross-
dressing, cross-age, cross-color, cross-species, mechanical—will be sealed in earnestness, forced to find these
practices meaningful, forced to assert that he and she indulge in these practices in order to find fulfillment.

And yet don't we really think that the one thing to regret in life is not to have dared, that the one thing we
will never regret is to have made fools of ourselves for
love and for sex?

Eroticism is something else. Eroticism is not satisfied in
contentment; it is the release of excess forces, craving extreme experiences in extreme torments and extreme
pleasures.

We walk the streets among hundreds of people whose
patterns of lips, breasts, and genital organs we divine;
they seem to us equivalent and interchangeable. Then
something snares our attention: a dimple speckled with
freckles on the cheek of a woman; a steel choker around
the throat of a man in a business suit; a gold ring in the
punctured nipple on the hard chest of a deliveryman; a
big raw fish in the delicate hand of a schoolgirl; a live
python coiled about the neck of a lean, lanky adolescent

Beauty and Lust

with coal-black skin. Signs of a clandestine disorder in
the uniformed and coded crowds.

These are very different from the suffused and anon-
ymous pattern of the erogenous zones we divine hidden
under the clothing of most passersby. These stand out,
blaze in the full public light of day. Objects of black
magic, they provoke effects from a distance, spreading
disorder in the programmed and urgent world of work.
We find ourselves obsessed by the odor of musk in the
wind rippling the waist-length hair of a cyclist, by a
crooked, sly grin on an ungainly and skinny guy. We find
ourselves disconnected from our role and our tasks, losing
the train of our thoughts, distracted by omens momentarily caught sight of. Signals of extravagances and reck-
lessness flash out of them.

Erotic passion is not an initiative of what we call our
person—our separate and discontinuous existence, source
of its own acts, responsible for what we ourselves say and
do. The structures and identities of our separate and discontinuous existence are forged in the world of work,
where every now anticipates an effect, a result, and subordinates itself to a now to come, where thought surveys,
calculates, and programs. The erotic object detaches itself
from the continuity of nature and the instrumental connections of the world of work. It maintains itself at a
distance from contact, closed in itself, an idol. It gives rise
to a longing to pour all we have of kisses and caresses,
the energies of our throbbing blood, the flash-fires of our
hyperexcited nervous tissues, the heat and phosphores-
cence of our carnal substance, into the other. This longing invades the inner fortress of our person and empties
it of the anticipations, initiatives, and identity with
which it had maintained its separateness. There is no
longer anything within us that surveys, programs, and
requires gain. An erotic object functions as the open gate

toward which the shock waves of our energies rush, to be compressed and intensified and inflamed there, and to break forth into the dazzling darkness beyond.

It can happen that erotic excitement is fastened on a whole human body. Apart from the pattern of lips, breasts, hands, and genital zone accentuated for sexual contact, beauty organizes the entire body into another pattern, linking up its contours, colors, and movements into a snare for the eye.

There is beauty and beauty. There is the beauty of perfection, that of a body integrally adapted to the purposes to which it is put. The beauty of an athlete or marine is like the beauty of a draft horse, exhibiting the engineering of limbs and muscles triumphing over the hardest physical tasks. The salient muscles of a ballerina are not erotic, even though the dance, contrary to work, is a sovereign activity having no significance other than beauty.

There is the beauty Immanuel Kant defined as that of purposiveness without identifiable purpose, the statuesque beauty of classicism, which is the object of disinterested contemplation. A young woman is depicted poised, self-composed, free, in a space emptied of any tasks or purposes for which her body would be molded and her limbs organized. A man is shown strong, proportioned, with graceful lines and a supple, sensitive, but inexpressive face, sovereign, ready for anything. Or they are shown with just a few objects about them, objects chosen for their beauty: an elegant young woman is gazing into a crystal brandy glass, the superb male is positioned on cliffs over the sparkling sea.

There is the beauty the Platonic eros contemplates, that eros that seeks immortal forms. The statues of the age of Pericles break with the distortions and grotesqueries of the art of Asia, India, Africa, and Mycenaean

Greece; they fix in marble perfectly proportioned bodies, whose symmetry excludes any disequilibrium that would suggest the possibility of internal breakdown or collapse. When they are carved in motion, their positions are so perfectly poised, their hands and arms so perfectly in accordance with the body's inner laws of balance, that movement, change, for them never implies the least lack of self-sufficiency. These bodies that look immortal, completely sovereign in nature, are raised on pedestals in empty space. The artists glorified and immobilized the triumphant bodies of Olympic athletes. They carved bodies, not fleeing dangers or hurtling their force against the blind inertia of things, but running with no other purpose than to display their inner mastery, held eternally in their eternally triumphant stride. The eros that chases after this kind of beauty is pursuing visions of immortality.

But what is erotic beauty? How does the beauty of a body detach that body from the contentment of our practical, expressive, and sexual couplings, and make of that body a snare for our lusts?

Ugliness is often the mark of fatigue and exhaustion. Utility constrains the suppleness and fluidity of the body. Women subjected to a factory job have a roughness, businesswomen brusk edges and crisp apparel that repel the wanton eyes of lust. The demands of work reduce the physical contrast between the sexes, so that the working woman is not an object before the man but a collaborator beside him.

The geisha and the temple maiden of the Hindus, Persians, Mayas, or Inca present the sovereignty of idle beauty, completely withdrawn from the world of work. Living in idleness, she preserves those soft and fluid forms of the voice, of the smile, of the whole body, that captivate without resisting what they touch. Her beauty does not triumph in the endurance of stern physical tasks; it does not endure; it is as ephemeral as the flowers that bloom in the night and die when the sun rises. She makes herself an object by covering herself with brilliant and fluid garments, jewels, and perfumes. The working man is stopped in his tracks, contemplating a body set apart, remote from his laborious concerns, ostentatious and alluring. Her sumptuous dress, jewelry of precious stones, plumes of exotic birds, and perfumes made of fields of rare flowers represent values, represent the dissipation of human labor in useless splendor. This intense consumption exerts a dangerous fascination. She tempts the worker to the follies and excesses of passion and dispossession.

Hers is not a body perfectly adapted to the functions of childrearing, or nurturing, or winning World Cup tennis. Not a woman who proves her intelligence in pursuing an academic career, a woman who demonstrates her integrated emotional composition, unblemished by erratic outbursts, in attaining to high political responsibility. A woman not striding in sensible walking shoes, but pirouetting in spike heels, or gliding in water-buffalo sandals; not wearing laundromat-washed t-shirt and jeans, but clad in the silk made by moths, with gold chains dangling in the sway of her movements or dozens of bangles on her arms. Not displaying muscled arms and milk-full breasts, but satiny breasts and a belly not destined for pregnancy and stretch marks. A woman who survives on celery stalks and champagne, or brown rice and water. She is not the female; she is the feminine, obeying aesthetic laws of her own making. An astral woman who appears in the crowd like a mirage, and who drifts effortlessly through doors to wander in rose-gardens and crystal pools created by moonbeams wherever she turns.

Beauty and Lust

The feminine form, which lacks the sense of heaviness that suggests the instrumental use of the limbs and the skeletal mechanics, whose ethereal shape is disconnected from physiological functions, is a vision of the woman disconnected from the biological female, the human animal there. But the designs of coral fish, the color-patterns of Himalayan pheasants, the spots of giraffes, and the stripes of zebras likewise do not outline muscle systems and internal organs.

Kant separated color from form in his analysis of beauty: color belongs to hedonistic pleasure in physiological reactions; aesthetic taste is a disinterested pleasure in form. But voluptuous pleasure is dispossessing, expropriating. The candlelight on the blush of a complexion, the hex signs painted on a face in black and scarlet make of a face an erotic object. Eroticism must sense the substance of flesh, and not only the outlines. The body's blood and secretions are visible in the lips, in the milky complexion, and in the dark and sultry orifices of the eyes. In her transgressive, tomboyish shape, there are the midnight skin and eyes of Grace Jones, on which sweat gleams rainbows.

The ethereal woman clad in grace would be insipid and unprovocative if her beauty did not at the same time suggest naked animality. We divine the cat, the bitch under the veils. How suggestive is her hair, right over the brain, which is incapable by itself of moving even one strand of it so much as a millimeter; the pelt in her armpits; the five million strands of down covering her body, each of which has only to be moved four ten-thousandths of an inch to make a nerve fire! In the woman we see the fox of the mescaline visions of Hopi legends. Our lustful eyes see under her beauty the tigress of myths, supernatural, casting strange spells into the stars of the night.

Beauty and Lust

The ethereal vision of the voluptuously feminine mesmerizes us because it breaks entirely free from the world of work and reason, where everything takes its meaning from something outside itself and is subordinated to the future. The consummate feminine look, Baudelaire said, is that blasé look, that bored look, that vaporous look, that impudent look, that cold look, that inward look, that dominating look, that voluptuous look, that wicked look, that sick look, that catlike look—infantilism, nonchalance, and malice compounded.[1] It fevers us with the craving to break out of our professional and practical world, to break out of ourselves.

We crave to break through the self-contained form in which the feminine is so utterly removed, not only from the world of work, but also from us. What excites us is to break through this jeweled mirage, though we sense that we will thereby join not in its radiant epiphany but in its decomposition.

The nudity of a temple maiden or a geisha, unlike the nudity of dancers and swimmers, is obscene. Before the curves of her idle muscles and the satiny softness of her skin, shielded from the sun of the working world and offered for touching and seizing, our lustful eyes also feel anguish and repugnance. They feel anguish before her nudity that—Marguerite Duras writes—invites strangulation, rape, ill usage, insults, shouts of hatred, the unleashing of deadly and unmitigated passions[2]—and they feel a vertiginous attraction for the muck and stench of the disordered organs and suppurating orifices that her soft forms and delicate skin hold so weakly. Voluptuousness plunges all that is infantile, feral, violent in oneself into another, seeking all that is frenzied, predatory, bloodthirsty in the other.

The tingling of a caress on our spine turns our bones into gum, and our sheath of motor muscles shivers with chaotic impulses like so much nervous fiber. The aimless stroking of a hand on our abdomen turns it into a gland or a heart palpitating with blood and frenzy. The lips cease to shape words in ordered sequences, the mouth babbles, giggles, turns into a wet and gaping orifice. The toes turned in the empty air no longer strain to support the posture and probe along flesh and into crevices like tongues. Glands stiffen and harden, becoming bones and rods. The eyes cloud and become wet and spongy; the hair turns into gleaming webs. Among the body parts tinglings, spasms, minute spiralings of life are teeming.

The caressing hands move aimlessly over the flesh in random, repetitive movements. The muscles tighten, harden, the limbs grope and grapple, pistons and rods of a machine that has no idea what it is trying to achieve. Then it collapses, gelatinizes, melts, runs. The trapped blood surges and pounds, the heat billows, the spirit vaporizes in gasps and sighs. In dissolute ecstasy the body that had become ligneous, ferric, coral now curdles, dissolves, liquefies, vaporizes, becomes radioactive, solar, nocturnal.

Orgasmic pleasure, the supreme pleasure we can know and the model for all pleasure, according to Freud, comes, Freud said, when an excess tension that has been built up, confined, and compacted is abruptly released; the pleasure consists of the passage into a contentment and quiescence like death. It is true that we tend to fall asleep after orgasm, but the voluptuous nirvana is not in the sleep. It ignites in the abrupt changes of state, the transubstantiations, that the orgasmic body undergoes. The body that sleeps is not inert, it is incandescent with the delirious aurora borealis that streams in its blood, sweat, and discharges.

The cadaverous bodies exuding smegmic and vaginal effluvia, musks and sighs, contaminate, animate the sheets, the furniture, the air with throbbing eddies of life no longer one's own. The furniture holds wetlands for lilliputian choruses of insects and unnamable microorganisms; musks and sighs excite protozoa teeming in the air.

The erotic frenzy sweeps its vertiginous way over barriers, plunges toward nameless, proliferating excesses of life teeming in orgasmic decomposition and contaminations. This zone of decomposition of the world of work and reason, this zone of blood and semen and vaginal secretions, of excremental discharges and corpses, this zone too of mushrooming eddies of nameless inhuman life, which fills us with exultant anguish and anguished exultation, is the zone of the sacred.

The sacred is not separated from the here-below of generation and corruption, beckoning from beyond as the figure of holiness, wholeness, and ideal integrity. From the beginning the sacred is in decomposition, is separated from the world of work, reason, and discontinuous beings fixed in their identity, by decomposition. The zone of the sacred is the zone of spilt blood, semen, discharges, excretions, which excite the transgressive and ruinous passions.

The sphere of sexuality becomes the zone of the sacred, where the world of work enters into decomposition, in the transports of eroticism. From the most ancient times, the sacred precincts were places of orgy and prostitution. In our times, the erotic is a tabooed and prohibited sphere, repugnant and exultant, a sphere of rapture, anxiety, and voluptuous oblivion.

Males in the Middle Ages became erotic objects in the ostentatious garb of knights, in tournaments taking place in an enchanted world of sorcerers, dragons, and rescues, and in the siren songs of outlaw gypsies, predators on the organized feudal world. The male erotic objects on the

silver screen are eighteenth-century cavalry or naval officers who gamble away fortunes, duel, and dance, and
bandidos or twentieth-century outlaws and high-society
conmen.

In Medieval times knights and janissaries partici-
pated in the nimbus of the sacred sovereign. The Jesuits
have made of religion the mirror image of the conquis-
tador armies. In our days of the conscript army, archbish-
ops and ayatollahs bless the weapons, and priests and rab-
bis accompany the troops on the battlefield to sanctify
their missions. The dress uniforms of conscripts on parade make them objects ostentatiously set apart from the
civilian world of work. The conscript army is the religious order of the secular state. Bandidos prowl in the
outer region of sorcery and necromancy, consecrated in
that other religion of amulets, talismans, luck, fate,
omens, curses, and spells.

The starched white uniforms of naval officers, with
their gold epaulets, and the hats, capes, and mirror-
polished boots of cavalry officers with never the least
trace of the muck of the barracks and the gore of the
battlefield, make them appear as astral men come from
the outer spaces beyond society. The impeccable dress
uniforms of conscripts on parade herald the nudity of
their bodies vibrant with abundance, ease, and inex-
haustible energy. The geometry of starched creases of
their uniforms effaces limbs made of laboring muscle
and the flaccid circulatory glands of their bodies. Their
gleaming weapons show that their bodies are those of
predator animals destined to tear one another apart in
wastelands. Nineteenth-century bandidos and twentieth-
century outlaws stud their black apparel with silver and
their bloody hands with precious jewels. Their business is
with corpses, the corpses they wallow in, the corpses they
risk becoming. Over this vertiginous abyss of the excre-

mental, they look with eyes that are not surveying tasks
and enterprises; in their eyes is that blasé look, that bored
look, that vaporous look, that impudent look, that cold
look, that inward look, that dominating look, that voluptuous look, that wicked look, that sick look, that catlike
look—infantilism, nonchalance and malice compounded.

Figures of transgression, they excite the lustful eyes
of careerwomen and dockworkers. The luxurious hair
of cavalry officers and con men, like the shaven phallic
skulls of conscripts and outlaws, their hirsute faces
and hairy hands announce the stallion, buck, and wolf
under the white jodhpurs, khaki or black trousers. The
looks fixed on them crave to tear voluptuously through
their parade uniforms and find the hairy animal hollows
with their disorder of secretions and discharges.[3] Fighter
pilots, infantrymen, con men, and bandits are erotic objects— obsessive objects for those who long for freedom
from their own identity and for the ecstatic discharge of
passionate energies.

There is no one ideal of beauty, Kant allowed, for sea
shells, butterflies, or furniture. There is an ideal of
beauty for human bodies, he argued, because in the
human being beauty of form is expressive of character.
The ideally beautiful human form expresses purity, fortitude, serenity—ethical concepts.

But eroticism is the abandonment of the carapace of
character. Are there not as many kinds of erotic beauty
in humans as there are kinds of beauty in sea shells,
coral fish, and flowers? And as many kinds of eroticism?

There are so many hot zones in the city. There are the offices, factories, hospitals, and construction sites. Our lusts
are aroused at the sight of secretaries stationed on stools
in front of computers and of linemen attaching high

tension wires on pylons. The lust that wrenches these bodies from the machinery of the laborious world may well be more violent than that which grapples for the ethereal and artful bodies of disco apparitions and military balls. Lust sees the fox under the starched white nurse's uniform, the wolf chained in the servile and machinelike labor of the construction worker.

Certainly we, and not only Jean Genet, cannot think of gangsters that prowl the underworld and murderers locked in cages without thinking of them as erotic objects. Convicts spend their time on death row reading piles of delirious letters from strangers begging to marry them the day before they are executed. Marguerite Duras's most passionate writings—*Moderate Cantabile, Ten-Thirty on a Summer Night*, and *India Song*—were such love letters.

In the film *The Crying Game*, the IRA militant falls in love with the sophisticated feminine beauty of the lover of the soldier he has killed. When she opens her gown to him and he sees a penis and hairy testicles, he wretches in the toilet. The transgression he had anticipated—taking to his bed the widow of the man he has killed—is abruptly revealed to be an even more extreme erotic transgression. This widow then kills his comrade-in-arms, the woman who had been sent to kill him, and he confesses the murder so that the true killer will go free. He will certainly rush convulsively to her when the prison gates are opened, like a moth to the flames.

People do not really go to the beach to swim laps, or to "work," as they put it, on their tans. We go to look upon the human bodies lying or strolling barefooted in the sands as we look at the carnal bodies of zebras in the savannah or at seals on drifting icebergs in the Antarctic summer. All that masochistic talk about the naked ape. . . . At the beach we think that Homo sapiens is really a beautiful species of animal too. Our eyes are drawn to women whose bodies are full, mature, healthy, whose legs are strong, whose torso is flexible, whose hair without permanent waves and lacquers is lawless and free like the manes of fillies. We contemplate women whose movements are not trained into artificially elegant gestures, whose hands are rubbing their strong bellies or waving off the flies. Our eyes are drawn to males whose bodies are not built by Cyborg machines, but are naturally, genetically strong, harmoniously muscled. Not parading to be admired, not individualizing themselves with eccentric facial expressions or studied gestures, they stroll by, oblivious to us, lost in the pleasure of being on the warm sands and in the sea breeze. They are deer who have strength and speed to pass through any obstacles in the forest, but who are now at ease in the forest clearing, occasionally prancing about or challenging one another to mock contests. We see all the physiological reality of the females' mammalian breasts; the cushion this animal carries with itself in the shape of its buttocks; the penis, that urinary and semenal duct, in relief behind the speedo trunks; the chest rhythmically heaving with breaths; the sweat. Eating not cuisine, but sandwiches and fruit brought in brown paper bags and beach food, they snack frequently, as animals do. We are enthralled with the animal splendor of a female body, opulent and exposing a sensuality without body armor, of a male body turning compact and fluid power in all directions, of the hyperactive energies of adolescents. In our obsessed senses and our thought subjugated to the tides of our instincts, the superbly bared animal body becomes an idol that mesmerizes the imagination and engenders private myths and pagan religions.

Finding ourselves drawn to such bodies, our erotic craving incorporates envy of them. We ache to be in the pack and to find ourselves possessed of undisciplined animal beauty. We long to surf the waves as they do. All the artifice with which we have tried to make ourselves beautiful, our cosmetics, our stylish costume, our elegant and mannered gestures, our coy and telling looks, we long to shed. We long to be a beach bum, an animal making love with them on the night sands. In such love-making, outside the network of rules that organizes the city spread behind us, they will lead us, as Friday led Robinson Crusoe to an elemental world made of sands, sea, and sun in Michel Tournier's novel *Friday*. Such lovemaking will find among them someone who, like Boddhi in the film *Point Break*, will go ever further from the world where grim androids locked in metal prisons drive the freeways, someone who, hunted from continent to continent by the FBI, will disappear into the hurricane of the century.

The flash-fires of erotic excitement are kindled by frail and fleeting epiphanies. You, the compleat suburbanite, white Anglo-Saxon Protestant, were in a corridor of the airport between plane changes, and abruptly an African woman pushed you against the wall and kissed you in the mouth: it electrified you for days like nothing your ever-available and compliant wife could ever do to you. How the carnal smile that waiter flashed you in Oaxaca obsesses you! How your body is blazing from that brief kiss the young Mexican salesman gave you in the dressing room of the department store!

Why is it youth that inflames the extreme emotions of eroticism? Unmarked by the furrows and wrinkles that aging will inscribe on it, it is the complexion of a Lolita that fevers our eyes. Youth is a transitional state somewhere between the milky cheeks of childhood and the strong and opaque colors of maturity. This ephemeral glow, precious and vulnerable, touches us tenderly.

As youth continues to mature, the girl will acquire the maternal pelvis ready for pregnancy, the boy the muscled body built by labor. The youthful form is beguiling, not because it is symmetrical and harmonious, giving the impression of self-contained equilibrium, but because it is undecided, open to multiple possible shapes. Plato is surely wrong: the beauty we love erotically is not a vision of forms that look eternal, offering satisfaction, contentment, and rest; we are captivated by the youthful, that is, insubstantial and vulnerable forms and colors. Every surge of passion is a transitory conflagration.

Most old people are not beautiful: bodies coarsened, potbellied and bent over for comfort and security, eyes leaden with prudence, lips shriveled with maxims of good sense.

Is your grandfather one of the beautiful ones? As a grown woman with a fiancé, you visit him, and now you embrace and kiss and caress him. As a boy you felt more sensual and languid in your grandmother's bosom than in your mother's. Grown up, you visit her, lying on her bed, unemployed, unoccupied, nothing but a woman, and those sensual memories come back to you so strongly that your adult male body is scandalously aroused, at the gates of death.

The faces of this grandfather, this grandmother no longer have the symmetry of classical models. But the geometry of shapes determines the cold beauty of buildings and champagne glasses, not the torrid beauty of erotic objects. The faces of Edith Sitwell and W. H. Auden, all in wrinkles, had in old age an erotic appeal they never had when they were young. Like your grandparents, their sly smiles, their surprise, their pleasure reverberate in all their wrinkles like sunlight spread in waves across a lake. The ephemeral character of these dancing pleasures in so thin and such frail carnal sub-

stance captivates you; you want to cover them with kisses
and caresses, sharing your springtime lust with them,
transgressing the taboos of incest and those put im-
memorially on corpses.

What unavowable and extreme emotions are aroused
by the old Maasai woman you pick up in your rented car
in Tanzania while looking for the lions of the Serengeti,
by the old Crow Indian with whom you share a naked
February night in a sweat lodge in Montana, by the street
kid sharing some ganja with you in a doorway in Calcutta!

The sacred is not only what sovereignly places itself
outside the world of work in sumptuous splendor; it is
also what the world of work and reason relentlessly
drives out, torments, and crushes. The delinquent, the
derelict, the senile, the lumpen proletariat—this living
human waste, more difficult to dispose of than the industrial waste of high-tech America—excites the most
vehement repugnances. The ethics that decrees that we
must treat each human as an end and never as a means
only, the religion that decrees that we must do to others
as we would have them do unto us, nowise restrain this
repugnance: the mobilized forces of religion have raised
the funds and organized the campaigns to elect the can-
didates who pledged to make room in the prisons by exe-
cutions and make room in the schools and hospitals by
massive deportations.

And then, one day, something catches your eye and
holds it in thrall: the California sunlight nestling in the
hair of an old Indian woman who walked from the killing
fields of Guatemala; the purple lips, soft as the petals of
an orchid, on the face of a Congolese child sick with
AIDS; a brief television image of the black waves rising
like sea snakes about the torso of a Haitian refugee in a
raft; a newspaper photograph of the face of a young Peruvian peasant who buried himself up to the neck on the

Beauty and Lust

Lima hillside to which the city fathers had sent the police and the bulldozers to clear away the squatters and their huts.

The frailty, the improbability of such apparitions of beauty churns strange storms in our loins. How we long to drop everything and cover them with all we have of kisses and caresses! In the decomposition of the world of work and reason, transgressive and ruinous passions catch sight of the sacred.

10

Joy in Dying

How visible is the fear in someone of our own species—
or of another species! How visible is the sense of being
vulnerable, the wariness of the mice in the cellar, the
forest birds, the vicuñas in the Andes, the clownfish in
the reef!

We who ceaselessly anticipate the future in every
move in our world of work cannot but anticipate the
calamitous violence of the death waiting to strike us.
We look with horror at an accident victim. The coffin is
buried and we go back to our workplaces; the death that
struck others is covered over. But in the darkness and
dead silence we sense the imminence of our death, reminded by the inert stones that pave the paths of our
workplace and by the dim air of threat in the sharp or
fragile, heavy or miniaturized, implements we have arrayed about us.

We who acquire individual identity in our work fear
for the security of our local field of work and reason.
This fear turns into an impotent anguish when we see
others using their reason to build the insane juggernauts
of war, which devastate the world of reason and oblit-
erate the future of all we work for. Our fear becomes
helpless dread when confronted with the tidal waves,
earthquakes, and volcanic eruptions that abruptly
plunge the works of labor and reason into chaos and
catastrophe.

We seek to contain our anxiety within the limits of
prudent fear, which measures our enterprises according

Joy in Dying

to the limits of our time and resources. Such fear gives a
sense of urgency to our reason and our work. Fear of
death accompanies our working lives as we realize that
they may be cut short in the midst of enterprises unful-
filled and causes unaccomplished. The black wall of
nothingness ahead darkens all the meaning we have
elaborated and are elaborating in our work. We seek to
ensure that others will take up our work when we can no
longer do it. We build a household for our children, we
transfer the management of our company to competent
and ambitious subalterns, we publish our speculations
and convictions so that the rising generation can use
them to build a better world.

There are people who die serenely, those who, in
Nietzsche's words, die at the right time. They die with
the sense of having lived their lives and having accom-
plished as well as they could what tasks they had set for
themselves with the forces and resources they had. They
die with the confidence of having left their accomplish-
ments and convictions in good hands.

When the dreaded comes to pass, our futile fear, anguish, and panic often give place to something else. The
striving and anticipation of our reason give place to observing the advance of the catastrophe with attention
and something like a fascination. People who have nar-
rowly survived accidents often tell of a strange, lucid
awareness of what is happening second by second, watching the inevitability of the impact, the adrenalin surge in
their bodies producing not panic or desperation but
rather a kind of intellectual lucidity, almost a curiosity.
People who undergo surgery or suffer ravaging illness
often watch what is happening to them with this same
strangely calm and attentive absorption, indifferent now
to the projects they had made of their lives.

Joy in Dying

There are also moments when we abandon the serene
pleasure of accomplishment in the world of work and
reason, yielding to a euphoria that surges in the dissolution of our skills and our individual identity. We seek out
the rock cliffs on the hills beyond our town, where all the
familiar streets of our life are no longer visible; we let
our eyes drift off into the inhuman and empty skies. We
feel insignificant and alienated; yet we stay, caught up in
shimmering winds. We feel the stable structures of our
skills and habits fading, our mental diagrams and maps
dissipating; we feel the name, title, profession, and role
we maintain in our familiar social world, these things
which give us a sense of a stable identity, dissolving in
the inhuman and empty skies. We sink into an anxiety
that unfolds as an inhuman exhilaration.

The exhilaration has an inner momentum that may
drive us to cliffs still higher and more remote, to the
Andes and the Himalayas. In the inner momentum of
the discharges of emotion—in which we feel the dissolution of our boundaries, our body armor, the inner framework of our skills, the hard shell of our character—we
sense cliffs ahead where we may drift away and never re-
assemble ourselves. This premonition does not detain us.

The euphoria we know in walking across Borneo,
in cross-country skiing the Alaskan wilderness, and in
ocean diving lies in having our eyes open to the mortal
dangers we are skirting. We do not speak of them to
those who do not go; when we tell our girlfriend, boyfriend, or parents about trekking in the Himalayas, we
do not speak of the dysentery or the risks of breaking
a leg days from any doctor or hospital; that is because
the only pleasure we can communicate to them that
they can understand is the grandeur of mountain vistas.
But among fellow-trekkers, at night in the camp, we

mention the risks, evoking them with only a few words, because they immediately understand. They have no anxious looks on their faces; they smile with shared elation. The moment when the path gives way and we plunge into catastrophe is anticipated with horror and exhilaration.

Every strong emotion whose inner momentum hurls it toward the unthinkable trembles with the anguish that anticipates death. Socrates defined philosophy as the overcoming of the anguish before death by an ecstasy of the mind that arises from the anesthetization of the body and survives its death. But in every exhilaration, we feel the anguish with which we throw ourselves into an abyss turning into delectation. In every exhilaration we sense the possibility that the final leap into the abyss will be experienced as joy.

Once we feel the strength that turns anguish into joy in dying, we are delivered over to all the joys that come in laughter rolling over our defeats and mortifications, in the blessing that greets everyone with passionate kisses of parting, in every love risked. The life delivered by joy from the fear of death would not be that of Socrates in prison justifying obedience to every unjust state and re-coiling from the miseries of exile. The clairvoyance that sees into the abyss will illuminate with its limpid light the nature of all human activities, both those that delude us into thinking that, guided by objective understanding, we can accumulate pleasures without torments and risks, and those that open to us the exhilarations of every exile. The doctor will know the anguish and the joy of his con-tention with the forces of invincible death; the musician will joyously sing the barbarian song that casts omens and spells unto hearts that are remote and silent; the thinker will know in his exultant upward fall the thoughts that flare and die away without accumulating representations.

The exploits of brave and determined women and men who prevail against great odds prevent humankind from sinking wretchedly into the resignation that the rich and the powerful assign to the vast majority. But heroes are not the strong who seize the opportunities that history momentarily opens. How many of those in whom we have found hope—Gandhi, Che Guevara, Martin Luther King, Malcolm X, Carlos Fonseca, Steve Biko—have failed! The heroes are hunted down by the KGB and the CIA, are assassinated in cathedrals and bludgeoned to death in secret dungeons. It is not because they succeed that they are heroes but because they laugh at death.

In that desolate advance of greeds and despairs, betrayals and complicities that is the history of our species, we hear their laughter. Their laughter blesses their comrades and all those who are downtrodden and tortured. Their laughter is heard again, in shantytowns and mountains far from their death, years after their death, in the powerful throats of those who continue to arise among us as heroes.

The guerrilla who joined the cause knew from the beginning that the struggle might fail, that he or she might end up bound to a stake before a firing squad. The knowledge of the justice of the cause, and the knowledge of the silent torment endured by those for whom the guerrilla struggles, shapes the laughter that will explode and the words of blessing and cursing that she will utter. But when she joined the cause she thought or believed that when that day came, she would laugh, she would be able to laugh. This inner strength to endure the sacrifice and to die laughing was in her before she knew the extent of the oppression, the justice of the cause, and the means of the struggle.

Something in her understood that laughter can come at the end of the plunge into the deepest horror, where she sees ever wider the extent and the viciousness of the tyranny, the further cruelties and slaughters that the struggle will bring to its intended beneficiaries, the uncertainty, even the unlikelihood of success, the vain death that may well come to her in a defeated cause.

Heroes are those who live and die in high mountains and remote continents far from our comfortable and secure rooms in the urban technopoles, where we meet to read to one another what we have thought out on our computers. Heroes extend the radiant heights and remote horizons for our best thoughts and longings. And there are heroes among us. They would laugh at the grandiose word. They are not on the barricades; they may be in hospital rooms dying of ravaging diseases. When we visit them, filled with guilty horror, their laughter incredibly dissipates our anguish. But those who really visit them, buddies, embrace the dying ones, cover them with kisses and caresses, laughing at the contamination they risk.

Is there something in us that understands the laughter of heroes? In the moment of shared laughter or weeping, there is a transparency among individuals, as if the emotional outburst gave rise to a single torrent surging within them. If we, who have not yet faced our death with laughter or with whimpering and cowardice, can venture to speak of those who laugh in the face of firing squads or with bodies swarming with deadly viruses, it is because language came into existence to speak of what we laugh and weep over together.

In the world of work and reason, every moment is subordinated to a future moment. The sense and direction of every present depends on a future, on a conclusion or result. But there are moments when the grip of a projected result on one's present eases, and the present lights up and burns in a surge of liberation and exultation.

When a sentence or train of sentences begins, it introduces a grammatical structure and a vocabulary that we comprehend by anticipating their development. As it continues, our anticipation of the full statement narrows and becomes more determinate. Then the sentence or train of sentences ends by abruptly flipping in a word from a completely different storyline, or the sentence breaks off in stuttering or gaping. What was anticipated, and our anticipation itself, collapse into nothing. This collapse of our earnest and attentive anticipation vacates the mind, leaving a pleasurable sense of release, and we break out in laughter.

At the moment when none of the anticipated words are there, we are held in the present, a present disconnected from the chain of word-vectors of the past and from the anticipated conclusion. We know a moment of release from our subjugation to the anticipating mind; the moment that was chained to future moments is miraculously liberated. Our laughter, in repeated gasps, holds on to that moment and reinstates it.

It is not the meaning of the word switched over from a completely different storyline that makes us laugh, for its meaning throws our mind into a new effort to retroactively reinterpret the sentence from the beginning, as well as to anticipate what follows. Words that are more meaningful, more significant than the words we anticipated provoke the mind to anticipate a further, broader

range of possibilities beyond the statement we had expected. The mind is subjugated the more, to strive more,
work more, to seriously survey the field into which the
sentence is leading it.

Our attention had been riveted to a sequence of
movements and manipulations that were constructing
some object, and then, at the final moment, the whole
thing collapsed or exploded. Our hands are left with
nothing; we find ourselves detached from the ground
along which we were prudently advancing. Suddenly liberated from the anticipated chain of operations, we
laugh or cry out. Whether we laugh or howl, our pleasurable release grips the moment disconnected from the future, and our gasps of laughter or our outcries jump back
to that moment, repeatedly recapturing the moment of
rupture.

When an unexpected result is more advantageous
than the result we had anticipated, it subjugates us to
the task of finding ways to put it to use. The abrupt re-
placement of the anticipated object with one that is useless or ruinous forces us to recalculate our situation. But
at the moment of collapse, our outcries can switch into
an outburst of laughter. It is midwinter; we carefully fit
our grocery bags into the basket of our bicycle and, in
first gear, head up the hill and down, and, when our
house is finally in view, we turn the corner and our bike
skids on a sheet of ice covered with light snow and our
groceries roll on the pavement in a mess of smashed
eggs, slicks of olive oil, and hissing jets of coke. Then we
see that the leg of the only trousers we have to wear to
the wedding tomorrow has been torn by the gears of the
bike. Our mind is vacated, of cautiously pedaling the
bike, of the meal we were going to have, of the wedding. We laugh—or cry out—with gasps that hold the

moment fast and return to it, to the devil's miracle.
What matters, what the laughter or the moans hold on
to convulsively, is the awful yet—in spite of ourselves—
marvelous moment when what couldn't happen abruptly
did. A sober, busy office manager slipping and sliding
across a waxed corridor sputters laughter, seeing her
own clownishness. If a painful fall chokes her laughter,
she will laugh later when remembering and recounting
the scene.

He who finds himself in laughter delivered from
anticipation and from subordination to anticipated results also finds himself delivered from his individual
identity. A bungler abruptly materializes where the ex-
pert thought he stood. While laying out the explanation, the explainer vanishes, leaving a clown, or rather
surrealist language, words combining of themselves.
He who laughs does not take seriously the death of the
individual he was. The worker laughs at the death of
the worker; the speaker laughs at the death of the
speaker.

The one who laughs at the death of the individual he
was is nowise trying to establish or extend his limits, or
prove himself. He risks death on pure impulse, an impulse that does not anticipate the consequences. Nonsensical urges break up ruminations and explanations of
people who identify themselves as rational individuals.
On playful impulse, laughing, she dives off that cliff
into the sea which, for all she knows, may conceal
jagged rocks just below the surface. On playful impulse
he drives his clunker twenty miles over the speed limit,
climbs up the old firetower or down the ancient mine
shaft marked with a "No Trespassing" sign.

The fit of laughter or outcries comes to an end. The
disconnected moment that laughter holds on to does not

evolve toward a future that would give it meaning. The present dies; another present is born. The worker finds himself alive again, after the moment of loss of identity; he at once anticipates more material, new tools, a future. The speaker at once envisions a conclusion and sets out to argue toward it. But they will play impulsively with death again.

It can also happen that the moment liberated does not immediately die when the laughter ceases, the future does not immediately hook on to the next moment, and the mind is not subjugated once again to anticipate and desire. The moment may liberate us into another kind of time, carnival time, where the moments chaotically grip us and are held by the most intense and violent emotions. This young man decided to settle in Lancaster County. He found a job pumping gas, studied carpenter's and electrician's manuals, and spent his evenings building a house. Then, one winter night, he woke to flames dancing on the curtains near the fireplace. Naked in the snow, as the flames roared into the stars, he howled and danced and laughed. He did not go back to his job in the service station. He stood in the road and put out his thumb. In the year that followed, he exchanged tall tales with truck drivers, cooked up qualifications for briefly held jobs, learned some derisive and tender Spanish from Mexican streetkids, danced the samba with strangers in Rio.

The playful impulse that risks death can turn serious when an outbreak of laughter or tears gives rise to an intense current of communication. It can become the unreasoned impulse to kill whatever oppresses us, silences our common laughter and tears. This impulse does not arise as a planned enterprise, a surgical operation, since it

plunges the hero to his own death in doing so. There is
something playful in this impulse too.

Nora Astorga was born into one of the richest ruling
families of Nicaragua. Ambitious and gifted, she went to
law school. Exceptionally intelligent and extraordinarily
beautiful, she was pressed with offers of positions in the
leading export companies. Instead, she restricted her
practice to defending those arrested by the Guardia Nacional of the Somoza dictatorship. The commander in
chief of the Guardia Nacional was General Reynaldo
Pérez Vega, a key CIA asset. In the prisons and among
the resistance, he was also known as El Perro, "The
Dog": he visited arrested subversives in their cells,
smeared their testicles with grease, and released his dogs
on them. From time to time, passing Nora Astorga in the
corridors of the courts, he murmured to her that if she
really wanted to help her clients, she could visit him pri-
vately.

One afternoon, upon leaving the court building, she
left word for him that she would be home that night, and
if he would like to visit her perhaps he might have what
he wished. He came, with his bodyguards, to her home in
the center of the city. She opened the door to him herself, clad in a seductive dress, and ushered him into her
sitting room where there were flowers and rum and
glasses on the table. She laughed as the bodyguards
peered suspiciously about the room. She poured him a
drink, tasted it, and passed it, laughing, to him. She stood
close to him and abruptly kissed him on the mouth. She
murmured to him to come into her bedroom and leave
the bodyguards outside. Closing her bedroom door behind her, she laughed and dropped her dress to the floor.
He embraced her and she pressed up against him, press-
ing her laughter into his mouth, holding his head tight

Joy in Dying

as the Sandinista slipped out of the closet and cut his throat.

Incredibly, she managed to leave through a window and escape from Managua. She could only leave her children sleeping in their beds. She managed to join the guerrillas in the hills. When, three years later, the Sandinistas entered Managua in triumph, she was made justice minister, and decreed the abolition of the death penalty.

Heroes do not merely occupy their minds with the oppression and misery of a whole people and derive out of this pity for others, felt as a personal affliction, the forces with which to anticipate a future and construct a strategy of liberation. They are those who understand not only the suffering of the downtrodden, but also their bravery. They have shared it on doorstoops, in dingy bars, on the docks, and in the fields where the Haitians, the Somalians, the Peruvian campesinos laugh. They are instinctually drawn to the laughter of those who labor without hope for the future, whose thought cannot devise results and products. They are men and women who laugh at their individual identity, and impulsively play with death. They are men and women of strong minds, who study the extent of the tyranny and the justice of the cause and concentrate rigorously on what will make the struggle successful. But they know that if that day comes when the troops of the tyrant surround them and proclaim victory, they will be able to laugh in their faces, because they have so often laughed with the homeless on doorstoops, with day laborers in dingy bars, on the docks, and in the fields. Their cause is not to enlist the whole people in the service of an idea that sacrifices the present to the future, only to extend the world of work and reason to

the marginalized, to those languishing in shantytowns
and adrift in the filthy nights of cities. Their cause
and their struggle is to think and work for a world
where the laughter of those on doorstoops, in dingy
bars, on the docks, and in the fields will be heard over
the guffaws of the rich and powerful.

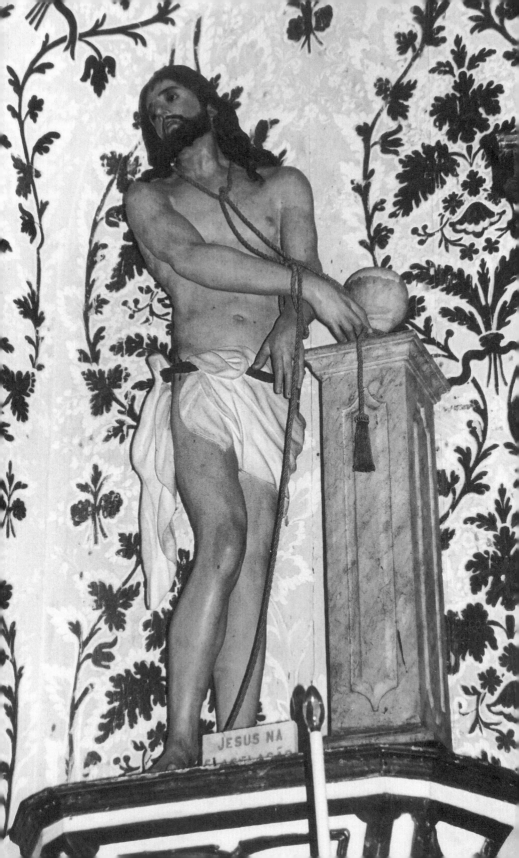

JESUS NA
FLAGELAÇÃO

11

Gifts

Near Jogjakarta a farmer I had come to know gave me a stone axe as old as the Java man. I marveled over the precise binding of rattan that held the blade to the handle, and over the so painstakingly sought-out jasper-blue stone of the blade whose form was perfectly symmetrical and whose surfaces were polished like the facets of a jewel. There was not a chip on the sharp edges of the blade: this axe had never been used. It had been a ceremonial axe, made as a gift to the spirits of earth and forest. Touching the wood handle and rattan binding, I discovered they had the grain and the form, but no longer the substance, of wood and rattan: the stone axe was petrified. Drawn from the earth and forest and shaped by hands at the dawn of human time, the earth and forest had covered it over, and made it yet more enchanted.

Every society that functions in its environment, that is not in a state of famine or siege, produces luxury objects. In societies with apparently the most rudimentary economies, we see jewelry that took amazing skill to make, intricately woven feather headdresses, ceremonial masks—objects made to be worn not for everyday use but in feasts and then thrown away or given to someone else.

Someone who buys up rubies, Persian rugs, or old masters and insures them or puts them in a bank vault as an investment is scandalously abusing them. The production of luxury objects is destructive of labor that could have been devoted to something useful. Anyone who squanders his wealth, pouring out champagne like water to his visitors or filling the bathtub with it for a woman he will know but one night in a country to which he will

Gifts

never return, understands luxury products. A man who
works hard and uses his wealth to purchase jewelry to
adorn himself, suits tailored in London, shoes handmade
in Rome, and a hundred-thousand-dollar sportscar,
which he drives cautiously and keeps in meticulous re-
pair, will be viewed by everybody as a poor fool with a lot
of pathetic needs. When he takes off his gold chain and
puts it on the throat of a waitress at a truck stop, when
he drives his sportscar at reckless speeds and can honestly
boast one day of having driven it into the river, he will
be seen to have soul.

The term *gift* designates events, apparitions, and
things whose grandeur and graciousness remove them
from practices of appropriation—from measurement,
categorization, and seizure.

It is not gift-giving to present your child with a base-
ball bat and uniform or a computer—things without intrinsic grandeur. They are things that everybody else in
his school has. They help him fit into his peer group, as
later the down payment on the house you give him and
his bride for their wedding helps fit them into the sub-
urb. The parents who give their son a car are teaching
him the rewards of money-making and corporate servil-
ity, and, since the car is as good as new, the value of skillful driving and attentive maintenance.

How different is a real gift! A few miles from where I
live is the Julian gliderport. The glider pilots sometimes
take passengers. One day I asked a friend if he had ever
taken a glider ride. No, he said, but his sixteen-year-old
son was taking lessons, and as soon as the son got his license, the father would be his first passenger. What height
of giving! Not just to pay for the lessons so that his son will
soar like an eagle, but to give him this gift of total trust, to
the point of risking his own life in his son's hands!

A gift is truly a gift only to the extent that, however
modest, there is an element of impetuousness, reckless-

Gifts

ness in it. Giving is a passionate act. Giving, by abnegat-
ing ownership of resources, puts the giver at risk. Every
act of giving already educes the passion to give one's life.

In the rocky summits of the Andes in Peru, in the
midst of a drought that has already lasted three years,
a young woman determines to descend to Lima in the
hope of finding some kind of work. No one in the hamlet says what all are thinking: that perhaps she will only,
can only, descend into prostitution. In parting with her
daughter, perhaps forever, the mother puts around her
neck a gold chain, the last thing she has that binds her to
the memory and touch of her dead husband.

It is not gift-giving unless what you give will come
into the life and heart of the recipient as a grandeur. It is
the extravagant and passionate heart that can recognize
and receive a gift.

Years ago, on my first trip outside Europe, I found in
the grand bazaar of Istanbul a copper bowl used for ablu-
tions and intricately inscribed with a prayer. The mer-
chant spun an enchanting and improbable tale over it. I
sent it to two graduate students who were close friends.
Now when I visit them and notice it on a shelf with a
few other objets d'art, I want to figure out some way to
get it back and give it to someone else. It brings me back
abruptly to the year when I first discovered the splendors
of Islamic culture and the Islamic soul. My friends teach
philosophy and live in New York; their travels take them
only to Paris every year or two. They had never, as I
imagined when we were young, wanted to discover all of
our world. On their shelf this copper bowl no longer pu-
rifies and sends forth and its prayer has been silenced.

Millions of tourists are flown from country to country, bused from temple to temple, landscape to landscape,
and return no more socially perceptive, more caring,
more awed, or more profound than they were before. On
the contrary, the trip, however prepackaged and handled,

Gifts

seems only to make them more attentive to discomforts and small aggravations.

All the paths up the mountain that imperialists called Mt. Everest but which the Sherpas call Sogarmatha— Sky-Mother—are now littered with tons of garbage. Kuta beach in Bali is now an Australian *zona rosa,* where white university students play frisbee and eat lobster to the din of the international best-selling pop CDs: the Balinese night pounds with disco amplifiers until the drunken dawn.

In the northeast corner of Turkey, in a place called Sumela, hermit monks climbed two thousand feet up a cliff face to a big cave strangely cut into it by some geological shift or miracle. Over time they walled in the cave and inside built a chapel and their hermit cells. For thirteen centuries young men came to join the cave-monastery, and when the Ottomans overran Turkey they did not expel the Christian monks; on the contrary, so great was their reputation as magi and shamans that every sultan came personally to offer them gifts. Only in the 1920s, during the war to drive the Greeks from Turkey, did the religious passions aroused cause the monastery to be vacated and its sacred objects to be desecrated and dispersed. When I came upon it, some twenty years ago, I was disgusted to find that the Ministry of Tourism had financed a road the length of the gorge to the site and had cut steps to the cave-monastery. And they were actually starting to build an elevator. Surely no one has a right to visit the monastery if he is unwilling to climb the perilous natural path the monks had found and used! One goes to a sacred place to change the course of one's life, to expose oneself to an oracle. The sincere visitors are those who have a life yet to live, who go at eighteen or twenty. Those who first devoted forty years of their lives to gaining security and respectability in the suburbs and in capitalism have something infinitely worse than arthritis now to keep them from climbing the cliff-face: a hardened heart.

177

Gifts

Gift-giving requires a specific kind of divination of
the individual human heart; it is not a matter of just asking someone what he or she wants. For a gift is not a
mere gratification of a need or want; it involves a
grandeur that can not be measured by itemizing one's
wants; it transfigures the soul of the recipient.

It could be that the recipient refused your gift or
buried it in a drawer, but that it was you who divined
rightly. You gave your son a motorcycle at the start of the
summer without telling him what to do with it, but how
chagrined you are when, instead of taking off for
Guatemala or Alaska, he just uses it to take suburban
girls for afternoon rides out of town!

Thoughts are gifts. They are not the categories and conceptual structures that are established for every practice in
society, for auto mechanics and nuclear physicists, psychoan-
alysts and political scientists, market analysts and literary
critics. Thoughts are illuminations. They are not formed and
fabricated by the abstractive, combinatory, synthesizing, or
metaphorizing powers of the mind; thoughts flare in immediate contact with the real. Skiing alone through the desolation of Antarctica, or spending a night alone in the silence
and dark of a cave, or contemplating the enigmatic shape of
the central carved stone called *intihuatana* in Machu Picchu,
or looking into the eyes of an eclectus parrot who is intently
looking into your eyes, a thought occurs to you, flashes in
you, and this singular reality is illuminated. There is no way
you can devise these thoughts; they happen, they are given.
They are the things your mind retains above all as the most
precious events in the stream of your consciousness. Unlike
conceptual schemes produced in the culture and picked up
by effort, you cannot recall these thoughts without feeling
an upsurge of gratitude. Each of us treasures a thought
someone gave us as a gift above all manner of material gifts.

After a day spent at the Plaza de Toros in Trujillo
in Peru, you visualized all the young men you knew and

Gifts

finally wrote to a student friend whose mind was brilliant
not in inventiveness but in sensitivity; he was specializing
in ancient philosophy. He loved the texts, learned Greek,
had gone to spend three summers in Greece. You thought
of him wandering passionately among the ruins of the
age of Pericles, his soul obsessed with epics of ancient heroes, his body slender, lithe, and strong. You told him he
should come to Peru and become a torero. You spent a day
composing and recomposing the letter, so that the sublime courage of the bullfighter and the fierce beauty of
the male glorified in the corrida as nowhere else in civilization were intensely and exultantly present to him
through the words of your letter, as they had been to you
in the fiesta brava in Trujillo. Before mailing the letter,
you spent two days locating the trainers and the ranch
where he could apprentice, and you added that to the letter. You wrote all this because he did have the tall, lean,
virile body, the natural sense of grace and style, and the
acute perspicacity essential in a bullfighter.

He did not come to Peru; he interviewed for a job in
Cleveland and spent the summer at home finishing his
dissertation. By the time you got back he was teaching
the thoughts of others and writing articles for tenure.

The act of giving is not a project of the giver. The
agent does not really give herself with and in her gift;
instead, not only the gift but the giving itself departs
from her. That is why we intensely feel that the existence
of the sequoia forests is a given in the planet and for us,
while there is no presence of an agent behind that forest.

To give an object or thought as a gift to someone means
that you no longer have any kind of proprietary rights over
it. The feeling that the giver is owed gratitude is the beginning of the debasement of the gift in a system of recompense with praise or honor, which partakes of capitalism, a
system in which not only is nothing free, but what you let
go of you do for profit. The mother who reminds her child

of the pain she suffered in giving birth to him and of the sacrifices she made to give him an education is demanding recompense. A wedding in which the father gives away his daughter and pours champagne to his guests like water is not an exchange but a potlatch feast. The mother who beams that she has not lost a daughter but has gained a son is not exchanging her daughter's help in the kitchen for her son-in-law's fixing of her car; she is joyous over having another person on whom to lavish her maternal love. In buying for them the house the newlyweds want, the parents delete their own wishes and taste. The giver must withdraw her name from the gift—to the point that the recipient does not know or no longer remembers who gave him this. Nietzsche wrote that whenever you do a good deed, you should take a stick and thrash any bystander, to muddle his memory. Then you should take that stick and thrash your own head, to muddle your own memory.

Receiving is as difficult as giving a gift. By deciding to make it in life by oneself, deciding to achieve and to deserve whatever one needs and wants, how many gifts one refuses!

How much is given on the planet, how much that is sublime! How much is not just the best on a continuous scale but is on a level utterly above all else, a level where things are incomparable with one another. The sequoias are not just taller than other trees, more exalted. You can't just say, "Well, I saw the virgin pine forests of the Canadian Rockies, so I got close to what the sequoias are; all I have to do is imagine trees taller still, more uplifting." When one day you get to the sequoias, you see the unimaginable. And then, incomparable with the sequoias, the baobabs await you in Africa, the banyans in India!

Among the sacred places one immediately locates on this transcendent level are Rheims cathedral in France, the Hagia Sophia in Istanbul, the temples of Khajuraho in India, Teotihuacán in Mexico, and Borobudur in Java.

Gifts

Anyone who has done it knows that it makes sense, if it is all you can manage, to save up for years in order to take off at least a few days from work and responsibility and fly to France just to see the Mona Lisa, fly to Japan just to spend a morning in the Ryongi Zen sand garden in Kyoto, fly to Peru just to spend, if that were all that was possible, a day in Machu Picchu.

There are transcendent encounters with living nature: the day you came upon a leopard, free, in the jungle in Sri Lanka, sprawled over the limb of a tree not ten feet above the ground, the leopard opening one eye when your feet rustled the leaves and then, with lordly disdain, closing it again; the night when, seated in a small whaler over shallow waters with pure white sand thirty feet below illuminated by the moon, you watched the sharks pirouette in the transparent waters under you; the day when, in the mountains of Nicaragua, you came upon the nest of a hummingbird in a cactus plant, woven of spider webs and containing one minuscule egg and one new-hatched hummingbird chick.

There are transcendent moments when fellow humans give us access into the hitherto unsuspected nobility that surges in our species: when the lepers of the San Pablo colony in the Peruvian Amazon gave a songfest and fishing hooks and two chickens to a young medical student named Ernesto Guevara; when Cheryl, who took the money they gave her when she was released from Long Bay Goal, bought a realistic toy gun, and held up the McDonalds in order to be returned to prison to die with Wayne, who has AIDS; when we see the beggar share some of his crust of bread with a vagrant dog.

There really are, in Salvador de Bahia, capoeira fighters lilting, sensual, and acrobatic. There really are, in Bali, women of consummate grace. There really are, in the corridas of Mexico, Peru, and Spain, toreros of breathtaking artistry and flawless courage. There really

Gifts

are, in Ethiopia, Nuba women elegant as gazelles, bold as lionesses. There really are, in Niger, transvestites beautiful as cobras. There really are, in the slums of Sâo Paulo, adolescents with fiery eyes and flashing knives, proud and beautiful as bandit chiefs in India's Uttar Pradesh.

There are transcendent collective events. There is anger spreading through the streets of Port-au-Prince in Haiti, anger marking in black the unallowable, the intolerable, anger that hurls itself beyond all that can reasonably be expected or demanded. This anger is the most precious gift of the disinherited to tourists and academics who have imprisoned their hearts through so many years of well-paid compromises and betrayals.

How many transcendent gifts we refuse! We do so by deciding for ourselves what we need and want. There are free and also professional counselors along the way, eager to help. Sly and treacherous they are, telling us to survey our personal needs and desires, and strengthening our self-assurance and self-satisfaction.

Such a system seeks to constrict us within every grubby act of will. The goal of such a system is to ensure that someone who thinks, "Well I do like this town and this cushy job gives me security," should understand that his decision also means, "I am deciding never to go spend twenty-four hours and see dawn, high noon, and midnight in the sequoia forest! I am deciding never to climb to Machu Picchu! I am deciding now to die without ever once seeing the coral reefs of tropical oceans! I am deciding now never to hurl a rock at a riot squad protecting the oligarchy!"

What gifts give is the ability to give gifts.

This was not understood by the charming and handsome student who had just graduated from your university and whom you ran into in Paris that summer. You took him to see Rita Renoir.

Gifts

She was performing in a cabaret in Montparnasse. In a
hooded black robe, she emerged; the light glowed about
her clasped hands. Abruptly the robe was flung off, and
a leonine mane hid her face, bent over her body in gro-
tesque and obscene nakedness. When she raised her face,
it showed the shame and malice of a little girl. Then
spasms of longing ravaged her strides. Hysteria raged in
her convulsed stomach. Her equivocal laughter rattled
against your ears. Milk and blood glistened in her breasts
and flanks. Her bared vagina threatened between powerful
thighs. Her sighs and hissings grappled at strangers in the
dark. Debauchery splayed her limbs. Terrible loneliness
shivered in her, blood-lust flared in her. Blissful and lethal
abandon made her weightless and floating. Her joy gained
speed, turning upon itself like a cyclone in the open ocean.

After an hour she climbed over the seats into the au-
dience inviting people to get on the stage, disrobe, and
interact with her. She spotted your friend, invited him.
He refused. "I will undress only before the one I choose,"
he mumbled to you.

But whatever could be wrong, you said afterwards, in
disrobing in front of these strangers in the dark, to
whom you would give the lustful pleasure of your body
without asking anything whatever of them, without
being able to recognize any of them tomorrow? What
could be more natural, like the sun that each evening
puts on its cosmic light show for whoever has eyes to see,
without asking anything in return?

It is not true that every piece of the planet would be
better left to nature, without a human being on it. A
human being is an animal evolved in the ecosystems of
the planet as much as the coral fish, the deer, and the
seabirds. Just as adding a bird of paradise to the jungle
destroys some things but makes other creatures flourish,
and complicates further the ecosystem, adding a human

dwelling to a piece of forest may preserve that forest and augment its diversity.

Years back I bought some seven acres of mountain land and started to build a cabin on it. But I lived in town and only infrequently went to visit the forest site. I never got further than digging a hollow on top of a natural rockslide, where I had thought to situate the cabin.

Bob was a graduate student in philosophy; having finished his coursework, he was now undertaking his dissertation. His wife Dee was a nurse. They had seen my mountain land, with its long-neglected cabin site. One day, they came to me and said: Give us ten thousand dollars and we will build a house there.

Bob remarked, with a laugh, that he had never built so much as a dog house as a kid. That winter I left the country. Bob and Dee went to lumber yards, talked with construction workers. Their ignorance and naïveté elicited offers of advice, of explanation, carpenters and plumbers even coming to the site on Sundays to look things over. When I returned at the start of the summer, I was astonished when I saw the secretive wooden dwelling they had built.

They spent the summer paneling the interior, installing electricity, plumbing, and a septic tank with leach field. When winter came, Bob stayed at a desk writing his dissertation, taking breaks a few times a day to finish some work on the house. By the following summer, the dissertation was finished and defended, and in September Bob and Dee left for jobs in Texas.

To whom would they give the house? Bob had worked as a teaching assistant; one of his students was Mark. Mark had no fixed major and was coasting these years of his youth. Once he moved to the mountain, he took a course in geology. As a project, he studied the geological history of the mountain where he lived. He came to

know the birds, the trees, the insects there. The next se-
mester he majored in geology.

Early the following fall, I had stayed out late one
evening. When I came home, I found Mark standing at
the door, haggard and in shock. He too had worked late,
in the geology laboratory, and then gone to the house on
the mountain. It was in ashes. The flames had risen high
before they were noticed from the valley below and the
fire department called. Arson? A dropped cigarette? A
faulty electrical connection? The inspection by the fire
marshal was not able to determine the cause.

When some houses burn, you think: That house was
old and, like one of us, it had lived a long life; perhaps it
was time for it to give place to something else. If a new
house burns, you may think of all the labor and thought
that the couple who built it day after day with their own
hands put into it; but you may also think that perhaps
they had invested too much of themselves in it; its burning may be for them a painful liberation of the soul. But
none of these things were true of the house Bob and Dee
had built and given to Mark, who was going to graduate
this year and give it to someone else.

I was rarely able to bring myself to go to the site in the
years that followed. I was never able to shape any ideas for
myself about what had happened. But finally one day I
thought: what am I searching for? For some answer, some
set of notions, some explanation, that would give me intellectual resolution and satisfaction, that would leave me
something more enduring and more appropriated than the
ashes of the house on my mountain land? Some return for
the gift that had not even been mine to give?

To accompany someone who is dying is the hardest
thing there is. Without being able to heal or console, we
stay with someone in pain and prostrate, someone mired
in a present without a future, someone who is going

Gifts

nowhere. To be admitted into the company of one who is dying is to risk our own integrity, our health and sanity, our courage. To be given the chance to accompany the dying is to be given the most passionate, the most extravagant of gifts.

Steve, trained as a philosopher, found a position as an adjunct teacher in London. He had also learned sign-language and volunteered to teach the deaf-mute. He decided to volunteer in London's buddy network, people who visit those who are HIV-positive as friends and are there to help as the disease pursues its fatal course. He was assigned to Patrick, an English teacher, who eight years earlier had tested HIV-positive. Within weeks, Steve and Patrick realized that they loved each other, but decided not to become lovers. Patrick had to prepare for his dying.

But shortly afterward Steve learned that he himself was HIV-positive. Four months later the first symptoms of full-blown AIDS appeared. He had but six months to live; more and more incapacitating infections repeatedly hospitalized him. During his last hospitalization, for a spore that had proliferated throughout his digestive system so that he was dying of starvation, he persuaded his mother to bring his father for a visit. A working-class man with traditional family values, his father had disowned Steve when, by learning he had AIDS, he also learned that he was gay. "My poor father," Steve said to Patrick, "really had no luck. He had two children; his daughter married a nigger, and his son married a man." Steve's last task was to make his father accept him, not because he wanted to die in reconciliation, but because he wanted to spare his father the guilt he knew he would feel when his son died. And he succeeded: in the days before his death Steve's father came every day, laughing heartily over Steve's real or imagined sexual escapades.

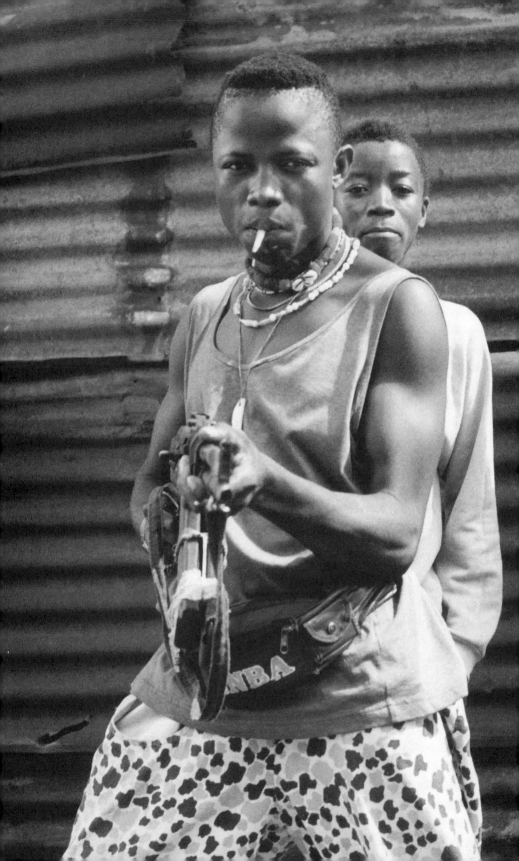

12

Love Your
Enemies

When humans armed themselves in the service of their
expansionist polis, nation, or religion, they rode thousands of horses to uncomprehending death. The vultures
came to bury their bodies in the sky. The Dutch, English,
French, Russians, and Peruvians sailed as far as To Pito O
Te Henua for slaves, and when these slaves sickened and
died, they threw them into the ocean, where the sharks
came to make them live again in their bodies. Today,
the homing pigeons and the dolphins, as conscripts of
human warfare, have been consigned to obsolescence;
human armies fly at stratospheric heights and their war-
ships stop far off in the ocean to launch the missiles of
destruction, and it is viral and bacteriological life that is
conscripted to spread the human species' hatred on the
battlegrounds.

The global, capitalist, free-trade economy now in
place guarantees that industrial powers will not again
wage world war against one another. They are disman-
tling their thermonuclear and biochemical arsenals. Instead, the Third World War their industrial might is
waging is a war on the world—on the great components
of nature: the fertile continents, the oceans, the supply of
fresh water (seventy percent of which is piled up in the
now melting ice of Antarctica), the atmosphere, the
ozone shield, the ultraviolet-reduced light that generates
life. The destruction of these components of nature since
the Second World War has already been equal to the destruction that a third, thermonuclear world war would

have wrought. Each year sees the genocide of seventeen thousand five hundred species of plant and animal life.

Justice is such an elusive thing of which to get any kind of concrete idea. In fact it seems to be a notion only hovering on the horizon, almost never at the center of any discussion. One first talks about how a social system works, a particular kind of market economy, the assignment of values to abstract things like intellectual property, the kinds and availability of education and health care, access to and manipulation of the organs of information and the expression of opinion, the migrations of peoples into a region, and the different economic niches the various ethnic groups have come to occupy. Justice seems to be both marginal and postponed, something to keep in mind somehow as the present economic and technological situation works itself out or evolves.

Human society is structured not only by the forces of technology and economic calculation; it is still also structured by political forces. The crucial force in political forces in human anger. Anger marks what is inadmissible, intolerable. Anger marks a refusal, a resistance beyond what resistance itself can reasonably accomplish. Anger empowers an intractable vigilance. Without anger, politics is influence-peddling and accommodation.[1]

In a working class barrio called Balconcillo, a youth has arrived at the threshold of manhood. He still has that vertiginous sense of how much his body has developed—his size, his voice, his hirsuteness, his musculature, his genitals—by contrast with that of his brother, who is two years younger. He has vividly felt, through his school years, how much his knowledge, his know-how, his thinking have changed each year, so that he has found it awkward and uncongenial to associate with students two years or even a year below him in school. New efforts,

new undertakings, new escapades, new thrills, beckon to
him each week. He has an intense sense of his past as a
succession of stepping stones he has crossed, and of his
present as open upon the paths of a future whose next
stages are already visible and beckoning.

Then the president abruptly shuts down Parliament,
arrests hundreds of opposition leaders and journalists,
and launches an all-out military campaign to extermi-
nate the armed opposition. For this young man, the horizons abruptly widen and he sees the field of his life
opening into the broad expanse of his prostrate country.
Everything he thinks of doing begins to take account of
the changes affecting his country. He knows someone in
the neighborhood who has contacts with the resistance.
He abruptly determines to join the underground. He will
fight, with all his strength, for the overthrow of the oppressor, for a renewed birth of his country delivered to a
stronger, nobler future by the arms of his united comrades.

He is instructed about the political and military situation, the possible allies and recruits, trained in arms and
sabotage. He does everything possible to conceal his activities and those of his comrades from discovery; he does
everything possible to escape from a raid unharmed and
unidentified, for his fundamental obligation to his cause,
even when undertaking the most dangerous of subver-
sive activities, is to preserve that precious and invaluable
agency of the resistance, his life.

But he is captured. He is tortured; he has done everything to stay strong, lest in a moment of weakness and
syncope he involuntarily betray his comrades. When his
torturers finally conclude they will get nothing from
him, they tell him he will be executed at dawn. They tell
him he has this night yet to save his life and decide to co-
operate.

The life he would save by cooperating is repugnant, inconceivable, to him. In the deepest core of himself, where he feels and knows himself best, he cannot imagine surviving by collaborating with the secret police, betraying one after another of his countrymen, forever distrusted and despised even by the secret police themselves. He will die. He does not suddenly give up the will to live and wish to die; but confronted with the inevitability of his execution, he no longer struggles to push off his death. He assents to his fate.

As he is led to the courtyard of the prison where he will be tied to a stake and shot, he feels a strange lightness. He is not standing on a scaffold before the people who will hear his last words of courage and defiance and will witness how he dies. It is dark and all about him the thick walls of the prison will muffle the shots. They will not be heard even by his fellow prisoners. He will be "disappeared." His mother will never be told by the police that her son had been captured. Yet, in the dark, he feels something like exultation: he is floating on light, as though the future and the past had fallen from him, with all their weight, and left these last moments disconnected, buoyant, and with all their energies intensified. Strange, miraculous buoyancy and lightness, miraculous elation as he feels himself falling, falling upward into the sky.

An individual "murders"; a society "executes." What do those of us whose society executes feel? With what dark and unavowed emotions are we drawn to the last days and last hours of the men and women waiting for their death sentence to be carried out? The total helplessness of the condemned man or woman makes us feel the exultation of power over him or her. Yet we cannot contemplate the condemned one for long without feeling an undercurrent of pity. The sense that we too are living under a death sentence invades us like compassion. But there is also the transport of erotic abandon in what we feel. For erotic passion is the exultation of a moment of time without resources or goal, without past or future. We cannot think of the condemned one without feeling a subterranean yearning to denude ourselves before him or her and to cover him or her with all we have of kisses and caresses. Men and women on death row, convicted murderers and traitors, guerrillas awaiting execution in the dungeons of Peru, Colombia, and Indonesia—what violent surges of passion they arouse in us! Because we do not bribe our way into their cells, tear off our clothes, opening all our orifices to them on the stiff cots or cement floors of their cells, our sensuality is constricted, asphyxiated, and ashamed.

Notes

1 The Navel of the World

1. "The mind in apprehending also experiences sensations which, properly speaking, are qualities of the mind alone," as Whitehead put it. "These sensations are projected by the mind so as to clothe appropriate bodies in external nature. Thus the bodies are perceived as with qualities which in reality do not belong to them, qualities which in fact are purely the offspring of the mind. Thus nature gets credit which should in truth be reserved for ourselves: the rose for its scent: the nightingale for his song: and the sun for his radiance. The poets are entirely mistaken. They should address their lyrics to themselves, and should turn them into odes of self-congratulation on the excellence of the human mind. Nature is a dull affair, soundless, scentless, colourless: merely the hurrying of material, endlessly, meaninglessly." Alfred North Whitehead, *Science and the Modern World* (New York: Free Press, 1967), 54.

3 Faces

1. Gilles Deleuze and Félix Guattari, *A Thousand Plateaus*, trans. Brian Massumi (Minneapolis: University of Minnesota Press, 1987), 180–81.
2. Ibid., 76.

4 The Religion of Animals

1. Friedrich Nietzsche, *On the Genealogy of Morals*, trans. Walter Kaufmann and R. J. Hollingdale (New York: Vintage, 1989), 72–73.

5 Blessings and Curses

1. Gabriel García Márquez, *Collected Stories*, trans. Gregory Rabassa and J. S. Bernstein (New York: Harper Perennial, 1991), 235–36.

Notes

7   Innocence

1. "After spending fifteen years of my life working closely with these patients, I think them the most afflicted and yet noblest persons I have ever known. Whatever 'awakenings' have been able to hold out for them, their lives have still been shattered and irreparably broken. But I have found singularly little bitterness in all the years I have known them; instead, somehow, beyond explanation, an immense affirmation. There is an ultimate courage, approaching the heroic, in these patients, for they have been tried beyond belief, and yet they have survived. Nor have they survived as cripples, with the mentality of cripples, but as figures made great by their endurance through affliction, by being uncomplaining, and undaunted, and finally laughing; not succumbing to nihilism or despair, but maintaining an inexplicable affirmation of life. I have learned from them that the body can be tortured far more than I thought possible—that there are some Hells known only to neurological patients, in the almost inconceivable depths of certain neurological disorders. I used to think of Hell as a place from which no one returned. My patients have taught me otherwise. Those who return are forever marked by the experience; they have known, they cannot forget, the ultimate depths. Yet the effect of the experience is to make them not only deep but, finally, childlike, innocent, and gay. This is incomprehensible unless one has oneself descended, if not into post-encephalitic depths, into some depths of one's own." Oliver Sacks, *Awakenings* (London: Picador, 1991), 288–89.

8   Catastrophic Time

1. Fred Adams and Greg Laughlin, *The Five Ages of the Universe: Inside the Physics of Eternity* (New York: Free Press, 1999).

9   Beauty and Lust

1. Charles Baudelaire, *Oeuvres complètes*, ed. Claude Pichois (Paris: Gallimard, 1961), 1256.

2. Marguerite Duras, *The Malady of Death*, trans. Barbara Bray (New York: Grove Press, 1986), 16.

3. "Sexuality, thought of as filthy or beastly, is still the greatest barrier to the reduction of man to the level of the thing. A man's innermost pride is bound up with his virility. The connection is not with the animal denied but with the deep and incommensurable element of animal nature. . . .

Notes

"*Animal nature,* or sexual exuberance, is that which prevents us from being reduced to mere things.

"*Human nature,* to the contrary, geared to specific ends in work, tends to make things of us at the expense of our sexual exuberance. . . .

"Our animal nature [has] its divine aspect and human nature its servile one." Georges Bataille, *Erotism,* trans. Mary Dalwood (San Francisco: City Lights, 1986), 158, 159.

12   Love Your Enemies

1. Jean-Luc Nancy, "La comparution," in Jean-Luc Nancy and Jean-Christophe Bailly, *La comparution (politique à venir)* (Paris: Christian Bourgois, 1991), 58–59.

Designer:	ReVerb, Los Angeles
Compositor:	Impressions Book and Journal Services, Inc.
Text:	11.5/13.5 Monotype Waldbaum
Display:	Truth
Printer:	Edwards Bros.
Binder:	Edwards Bros.